Δ The Triangle Papers: 43

KEEPING THE PEACE IN THE POST-COLD WAR ERA: STRENGTHENING MULTILATERAL PEACEKEEPING

A Report to
The Trilateral Commission

Authors: JOHN ROPER
Director, Institute for Security Studies,
Western European Union, Paris;
former Member of the British Parliament

MASASHI NISHIHARA
Professor of International Relations,
National Defense Academy, Yokosuka

OLARA A. OTUNNU
President, International Peace Academy, New York;
former Ugandan Ambassador to the United
Nations; former Foreign Minister of Uganda

ENID C.B. SCHOETTLE
Senior Fellow and Director of the Project on
International Organizations and Law,
Council on Foreign Relations, New York

published by
The Trilateral Commission
New York, Paris and Tokyo
1993

Library of Congress Cataloging-in-Publication Data

Keeping the Peace in the Post-Cold War Era: Strengthening
    Multilateral Peacekeeping: a report to the Trilateral Commission/
    John Roper... [et. al.].

        p. cm. — (The Triangle papers : 43)
ISBN 0-930503-70-8: $12.00
1. Peace. 2. Security. 3. United Nations.
I. Roper, John, 1935- . II. Trilateral Commission. III. Series.
JX1954.K345 1993
327.1'72—dc20   93-30079
                                                       CIP

Manufactured in the United States of America

THE TRILATERAL COMMISSION

345 East 46th Street	c/o Japan Center for	35, avenue de Friedland
New York, NY 10017	International Exchange	75008 Paris, France
	4-9-17 Minami-Azabu	
	Minato-ku	
	Tokyo, Japan	

The Authors

JOHN ROPER, in 1990, became the first Director of the Institute for Security Studies of the Western European Union in Paris. A graduate of Oxford University and a Harkness Fellow at the University of Chicago, he taught Economics at the University of Manchester from 1962 to 1970. Mr. Roper was elected to Parliament in 1970, and served until 1983. He was Opposition Front Bench spokesman on defence in 1979-81; and Social Democrat Chief Whip in 1981-83. In 1973-80 he was a member of the Western European Union Assembly and Chairman of its Committee on Defence Questions and Armaments; and was Chairman of the Labour Committee for Europe in 1976-80. After leaving Parliament, Mr. Roper was at the Royal Institute of International Affairs as Head of the International Security Programme and Editor of *International Affairs* (1983-90). Among his published works are *The Future of British Defence Policy* (1985), and companion volumes on *British-German Defence Cooperation* (1988, edited with Karl Kaiser) and *Franco-British Defence Cooperation* (1989, editor).

MASASHI NISHIHARA is Professor of International Relations at Japan's National Defense Academy. After graduating from the Law Department of Kyoto University in 1962, he received his M.A. and Ph.D. in political science from the University of Michigan. He has been associated with Kyoto University's Center for Southeast Asian Studies in Jakarta, and has taught at Kyoto Sangyo University. He has been a Visiting Research Fellow at Australian National University, Canberra (1979) and at the Rockefeller Foundation in New York City (1981–82). He is currently a Research Associate of the Research Institute for Peace and Security, Tokyo. Prof. Nishihara also serves on the Council of the International Institute for Strategic Studies, London. He is the author of many works on Japanese security issues and international relations, including *Promoting Partnership: Japan and Europe* (1982), *East Asian Security and the Trilateral Countries* (1985), *Senryaku Kenkyu no Shikaku* [An Angle on Strategic Studies] (1988), "New Roles for the Japan–U.S. Security Treaty" (1991), and "Transformation of Northeast Asia and Japanese Security" (1993).

OLARA A. OTUNNU is President of the International Peace Academy in New York. Born in Uganda, he was educated at King's College in Budo, Makerere University in Kampala, Oxford University and Harvard University, at which he was a Fulbright Scholar. Mr. Otunnu practiced law as an Associate with the law firm of Chadbourne and Parke in New York, and was also Assistant Professor of Law at Albany Law School. He was a member of the Uganda National Consultative Council, the Interim Parliament (1979-80), before becoming Uganda's Permanent Representative to the United Nations from 1980 to 1985. During his tenure at the United Nations, he served variously as President of the Security Council, Vice President of the UN General Assembly, Chairman of the UN Commission on Human Rights and Chairman of the Contact Group for Global Negotiations. Returning to Uganda in 1985, Mr. Otunnu was his country's Minister of Foreign Affairs until 1986. From 1986 to 1989 he lived in Paris, where he was Visiting Fellow at the Institut Français des Relations Internationales (IFRI) and Visiting Professor at the American University. He is presently a member of the Commission on Global Governance. He serves on the boards of several organizations, including the Aspen Institute, Aspen Italia, and Hampshire College.

ENID C.B. SCHOETTLE is Director of the Project on International Organizations and Law and Senior Fellow at the Council on Foreign Relations in New York. Prior to joining the Council, she was Director of the International Affairs Program of the Ford Foundation for ten years. Dr. Schoettle holds a Ph.D. in Political Science from the Massachusetts Institute of Technology and an A.B. from Radcliffe College. She is a member of the Academic Council on the United Nations System; the American Society of International Law; the Aspen Strategy Group; the Council on Foreign Relations; the International Institute of Strategic Studies; the International Studies Association; the United Nations Association of the U.S.A.; and Women in International Security. She serves on the Board of Trustees of the Henry L. Stimson Center and of the Scientists' Institute for Public Information; the International Advisory Board of the Institute on Global Conflict and Cooperation, University of California; the Board of Visitors of the Mershon Center, Ohio State University; and the International Association of University Presidents/United Nations Commission on Arms Control Education.

The Trilateral Process

Each of the four central chapters of the report which follows is the responsibility of its individual author. John Roper served as leader of the project and supervised the preparation of the introductory and concluding chapters.

This project followed up one element of the broader "Shared Security Responsibilities" working group that functioned under the auspices of the Trilateral Commission in 1991-92. John Roper also led that group, and prepared a paper drawing on its work for the April 1992 annual meeting of the Trilateral Commission in Lisbon.

Although only the authors are responsible for the analysis and conclusions in their individual chapters, they have been aided in their work by a number of others, notably in the workshop the authors held in New York City on December 19-20, 1992. The participants in that workshop, who spoke for themselves as individuals and not as representatives of any institutions with which they were associated, included: William BARTON, former Canadian Ambassador to the United Nations; Georges BERTHOIN, Honorary European Chairman of the Trilateral Commission; Richard N. GARDNER, Henry L. Moses Professor of Law and International Organization at Columbia University; Edward C. LUCK, President of the United Nations Association of the United States; Alex MORRISON, Executive Director of the Canadian Institute of Strategic Studies; Joseph S. NYE, Jr., Director of the Center for International Affairs and Clarence Dillon Professor of International Affairs at Harvard University; Robert ROSENSTOCK, Counsellor at the United States Mission to the United Nations; and George WARD, Jr., U.S. Principal Deputy Assistant Secretary of State for International Organization Affairs.

In meetings in Paris on March 8 and London on March 9, 1993, John Roper consulted with Trilateral Commission members and several experts, including Philippe DELMAS, Advisor to the French Minister of Foreign Affairs; Dominique MOISI, Deputy Director of French Institute for International Relations (IFRI); and Mark PELLEW of the Foreign and Commonwealth Office in London. In Bonn on March 10 Mr. Roper consulted with Gen. Klaus NAUMANN, Generalinspekteur of the Bundeswehr and with three Members of the Bundestag who are spokesmen for their respective parties—Karsten VOIGT, SPD Spokesman on Foreign Affairs; Werner HOYER, FDP Spokesman on Defense; and Karl LAMERS, CDU/CSU Spokesman on Foreign Affairs. In addition, Karl KAISER, Director of the Research Institute of the German Society for Foreign Affairs, hosted a luncheon including a range of other experts.

Indispensable assistance in coordinating the collection of pertinent materials for Masashi Nishihara was provided by Makito NODA of the Trilateral Commission Japanese staff. Nicholas SWALES, Executive Assistant for the Canadian Group of the Trilateral Commission, prepared a memorandum and provided materials about Canada for Prof. Nishihara. Materials about some European countries were provided by Ellmann ELLINGSEN, Secretary of the Norwegian Atlantic Committee, and Karel VOSSKUHLER of the Dutch Foreign Ministry. Prof. Nishihara also wishes to acknowledge the cooperation of the British, Danish, Norwegian, Spanish and Swedish embassies in Tokyo. He was also helped by Charles E. MORRISON, Director of the Program on International Economics and Politics at the East-West Center in Hawaii and Senior Research Associate at the Japan Center for International Exchange in Tokyo.

Enid Schoettle wishes to thank Sir Brian URQUHART, Scholar-in-Residence at the Ford Foundation and Staff Director of the Independent Advisory Board on UN Financing, for his help on this project; Lawrence L. HAMLET and Jennifer L. HOBBS, her two program assistants at the Council on Foreign Relations, for their invaluable research assistance; and a number of interviewees in the UN Secretariat and in various national missions to the UN for their insights and suggestions.

Olara Otunnu wishes to acknowledge the invaluable assistance provided by Ms. Nishkala SUNTHARALINGAM in the preparation of his chapter.

A full draft of this report was the basis for a discussion at the 1993 annual meeting of the Trilateral Commission, held on March 27-29 in Washington, D.C. Final revisions before publication followed the Washington meeting. The Nishihara chapter was completed in April, the Roper chapter in May, and the Otunnu and Schoettle chapters in July.

The Commission wishes to thank the Henry Luce Foundation and the General Electric Foundation for their generous support of this project.

Table of Contents

List of Tables and Figures

I. Introduction

The end of the Cold War lifts a central obstacle to the strengthening of multilateral peacekeeping and the extension of multilateral operations beyond traditional peacekeeping tasks. A revived United Nations Security Council and energetic Secretary-General are the global center of this rapidly evolving effort, but the passing of the Cold War also brings other institutions into the picture in different ways. The use of NATO as an executing agent for the United Nations in implementing the "no-fly zone" in Bosnia-Herzegovina is but one remarkable example.

The strengthening of multilateral peacekeeping is in the broad interest of the Trilateral countries. The new era we are all entering is so far one in which disorder is spreading in many corners of the world, and multilateral frameworks, in one way or another, often provide useful frameworks in which to address one or another conflict situation. Beyond particular conflict situations, strengthening multilateral peacekeeping will be important for Trilateral countries in developing post-Cold War cooperation with Russia and China through the United Nations Security Council, and with Russia and other former Soviet republics in frameworks such as NACC (North Atlantic Cooperation Council) and CSCE. It will be of major importance in sustaining and adjusting the security partnership among the Trilateral countries themselves, including adjustments in the roles of Germany and Japan and in the role of the United States.

A number of current peacekeeping operations are faltering. Part of the problem is that public opinion and governments have been calling for additional, ambitious multilateral operations—notably in the framework of the United Nations—without providing the resources and nurturing the structures that can sustain these operations over time. If allowed to continue over time, this gap between what the UN is asked to provide and what it can do could have disastrous consequences for the very multilateral frameworks which Trilateral countries—to which this report is primarily addressed—say they want to strengthen.

The extension of multilateral operations beyond the traditional UN peacekeeping tasks of the Cold War era is also proving to be more complicated and dangerous than some had imagined. United Nations Under-Secretary-General Marrack Goulding, in remarks to the Trilateral Commission annual meeting at which a draft of this report was discussed, set out three conditions that must exist for a proposed peacekeeping operation to succeed: "(1) the mandate or task for the peacekeeping operation must be clear, practicable and accepted by the parties; (2) the parties must pledge themselves to cooperate with the peacekeepers and those pledges must be credible; (3) the Member-States of the United Nations must be ready to provide the human and material resources needed to do the job." As he also noted, "on any particular day only a minority of the actual or potential conflicts in the world fulfill those conditions."

In sum, strengthening multilateral peacekeeping in the post-Cold War era will not happen automatically. Strengthening UN and other multilateral frameworks is not a means for Trilateral and other governments to avoid their responsibilities, but rather a useful means in many conflict situations for meeting those responsibilities in a shared manner.

The four central chapters of this report address particular aspects of the challenge. John Roper focuses on the widening range of tasks being organized under the broad rubric of multilateral peacekeeping, and proposes improvements in arrangements for deploying forces. Enid Schoettle's chapter concentrates on the financing of peacekeeping, and how it should be improved. Masashi Nishihara asks what more particular Trilateral countries can bring to the effort—and what challenges they face in doing so. Olara Otunnu's chapter is concerned with maintaining the broad legitimacy of United Nations action. A brief final chapter draws together recommendations from the four central chapters and offers a few concluding comments. The address which Marrack Goulding gave to the Commission is published as an appendix.

II. A WIDER RANGE OF TASKS

John Roper

A. THE RETURN OF COLLECTIVE SECURITY AND THE EXPANSION OF UNITED NATIONS TASKS

In 1945 the founding members of the United Nations wanted to make it an effective instrument of collective security and to avoid the problems that had beset the League of Nations. The international community gave the United Nations the authority through the Security Council to identify states guilty of aggression and then take action to force them to withdraw and be punished. It was a form of collective security with significant limitations because the five permanent members of the Security Council protected themselves by their veto rights; it was collective security imposed by the most powerful on the less powerful.

The ideological conflict of the Cold War led to a prolonged deadlock in the Security Council and prevented the mechanism of enforcement operating. Instead, Lester Pearson and Dag Hammarskjöld invented the softer option of UN peacekeeping. This accepted that (as agreement could not be reached as to who was guilty) punishment was ruled out. UN Blue Helmets would be put in to freeze a conflict situation and keep the parties apart. Many of these units have been in position for decades—in Cyprus, in South Lebanon, in the Golan Heights—keeping a situation from exploding while desultory negotiations continue.

The end of the Cold War and the more cooperative environment in the Security Council has not only seen a return to collective security and the reversal of aggression in the case of the Iraqi attack on Kuwait, but also a rapid increase in the tasks for which UN forces have been used. The number of forces deployed has quintupled since mid-1991, but more importantly their roles have widely expanded. They are no longer seen as being in place merely to freeze a situation, in the essentially passive role of maintaining a cease-fire. They are playing a part in a much more active process of peace-building—to handle national reconstruction, to facilitate a transition to a democratic government, to provide humanitarian assistance, to assure the return of victims of war and refugees. Such "second generation" peacekeeping forces are seen as being in place for much shorter periods, at least at the time when they are initially authorized.

This process of making fuller use of the machinery of the United Nations has presented its own problems—a number of which are addressed in this report—and inevitably there have been disappointments and setbacks when the United Nations has not been able to respond fully to the demands placed on it. The first and so far most successful of these new types of deployments was the UN's action in Namibia. The actions in Cambodia, Angola, El Salvador, the Western Sahara, Croatia, Bosnia, Somalia and Mozambique have also demonstrated that UN actions are now multifaceted with a range of objectives.

These new more creative roles which UN forces are being asked to undertake are intended to support long-term solutions to problems. They are more complicated than either identifying an aggressor and punishing him or alternatively putting peacekeepers in to maintain the status quo. The instruments used need to include political, economic, humanitarian and military levers; and while the last is the one to which most attention is given in this report, military action must be seen as part of a complex process of crisis management and peace-making in which a variety of instruments will be necessary. One of the problems of the new situation is that these multiple tasks given to UN forces by the international community are not always mutually compatible.

In his report *An Agenda for Peace* issued in June 1992, the Secretary-General of the United Nations, Dr. Boutros Boutros-Ghali, sets out a structure for examining the new dynamic approaches to preventive diplomacy, peace-making, peacekeeping and peace-building expected of the United Nations. In practice developments have run ahead of the consideration of this report, with the world's crisis regions demanding responses from the international community. The responses that have been developed to deal with particular situations are themselves creating the precedents on which future actions will be built. In time a new well-ordered structure may appear, but meanwhile we will have a less than tidy set of arrangements which have been put together to deal with particular situations.

While the experience of the last two years has permitted the United Nations to develop in ways that were not thought possible for most of the forty-eight years since its creation, it would be wrong for our countries to assume that the more cooperative attitude within the Security Council cannot be reversed, that we now live in a veto-free world.[1] The Permanent Members of the Security Council do not actually have to cast their vetoes in a public session of the Council for their influence to be felt. It is nonetheless important to maintain as wide a consensus as possible within the Security Council and within the United Nations as a whole if these instruments are going to continue to be effective. The Trilateral countries may find this process of consensus-building within the UN unduly protracted and sometimes politically frustrating, but there would be very considerable costs in abandoning it.

B. ADAPTING REGIONAL ORGANIZATIONS CENTERED ON EUROPE

The Charter of the United Nations gives regional organizations a role within the arrangements for maintaining international peace and security. The primacy of the United Nations is made clear in the Charter by Article 53 which lays down that no enforcement action—no use of military forces without the consent of the states concerned—shall be taken by a regional organization without the authorization of the Security Council. On the other hand Article 52 states that members of the United Nations "shall make every effort to achieve pacific settlements of local disputes through such regional arrangements or by such regional agencies before referring them to the Security Council." There is therefore a clear distinction between actions taken with the consent of the states concerned (where the Charter encourages regional bodies to try to solve problems in their own regions) and those where action, including military action, is imposed upon states without their consent (where the Security Council has the sole right to authorize action).[2]

Although the Charter is not explicit, regional bodies have traditionally been seen as having a role in solving problems among their own members. They were seen as providing a measure of regional collective security. In the Cold War period in Europe another kind of regional organization developed, explicitly for collective self-defense against an outside attack. Western European Union (WEU) and the North Atlantic Treaty Organization (NATO) were organizations of this sort. They based themselves not on Article 52 or Article 53 of the Charter (Chapter VIII) but on the earlier Article 51 which makes clear that "Nothing in the present Charter shall impair the inherent right of individual or collective self-defense if an armed attack occurs against a member of the United Nations, until the Security Council has taken measures necessary to maintain international peace and security." The existence of this right was of great importance at a time when the Security Council was immobilized by the Cold War.

In both the 1948 Brussels Treaty that created WEU and the 1949 Washington Treaty that created NATO, the key articles which provide the security guarantees on which these military alliances are based make explicit reference to this provision of the UN Charter and accept the obligation to report any action taken in collective self-defense to the Security Council and terminate it as soon as the Security Council has taken the measures necessary to maintain or restore international peace and security.

The end of the Cold War has led to a reappraisal of security arrangements in Europe and an examination of the way in which the various structures built to deal with the Cold War could be adapted to the new situation. As Europe failed in the second half of 1991 to find satisfactory answers to the deteriorating situation in Yugoslavia this became more and more urgent. From an early stage the Conference on Security and Cooperation in Europe (CSCE), the twenty-year-old body which provided a framework for dialogue and negotiation during the closing stages of the Cold War, was seen as an important regional framework. Various governments proposed the transformation of the CSCE into the sort of regional arrangement referred to in the UN Charter with the power to authorize peacekeeping operations in the case of disputes among its members.

CSCE's geographic breadth makes it in some ways a somewhat unusual regional arrangement. Its 53 members include all NATO members, the European neutrals, the former members of the Warsaw Pact and the fifteen republics which have emerged from the former

Soviet Union. Japan since 1992 enjoys a special observer status. CSCE is also unusual in that four of the five Permanent Members of the Security Council are members. It is however a body with only embryonic institutional structures and with no experience in conducting military operations.

Much of the first half of 1992 was spent in trying to find how the framework of the CSCE could be linked both to the United Nations and to the more developed but less geographically comprehensive Western organizations—the European Community, NATO and WEU. These three bodies were also developing.

The European Community had, with the "blessing" of the CSCE, dispatched monitors to Yugoslavia in July 1991, and established a Peace Conference on Yugoslavia under Lord Carrington. Later that year the Treaty on European Union signed at Maastricht agreed on the need for a Common Security and Foreign Policy with a potential defense dimension.

NATO has taken a series of steps to ensure that the experience, expertise and resources which it had developed during the Cold War could be applied to the new security challenges in Europe. In December 1991, it created the North Atlantic Cooperation Council (NACC) which provides a framework for dialogue with its former adversaries in the Warsaw Pact and successor republics of the Soviet Union.

While there has been wide agreement among the member states of NATO on the need to maintain it as a structure for transatlantic security cooperation, there has not always been agreement as to how it should adjust to take on new functions, particularly if these extend outside the boundaries of its member states. However on 4th June 1992 NATO Ministers meeting in Oslo were able to agree that they were "prepared to support, on a case-by-case basis in accordance with our own procedures, peacekeeping activities under the responsibility of the CSCE, including by making available Alliance resources and expertise."

Western European Union, which although older than NATO had played a relatively passive role during most of the Cold War, was given a new impetus by the provisions of the Maastricht Treaty on European Union and the decisions of its own nine members[3] to give it a more operational role. This was marked by their Foreign and Defense Ministers deciding at a meeting in Bonn on 18th June 1992 on the use of the forces that their member states would make available to WEU. They agreed that their forces could be used to support "the effective implementation of conflict prevention and crisis management measures including peacekeeping activities of the CSCE or the United Nations Security Council." At this stage WEU's ministerial mandate included action for the UN as well as the CSCE, while NATO was limited to the CSCE; but this distinction was removed on 17th December 1992 when NATO Ministers meeting in Brussels also confirmed that their organization could work directly for the UN.

The decisions made by the NATO and WEU Ministerial meetings in June 1992 paved the way for the decisions taken by the CSCE at its Summit Meeting in Helsinki on 10th July 1992. It agreed that CSCE should aim to become a regional arrangement[4] in the terms of Chapter VIII of the United Nations Charter. There was also in the final document agreed by the CSCE Helsinki Summit Meeting an extended section on how the CSCE could be developed in order to fulfill a more effective role in conflict prevention and crisis management in Europe. This provides for peacekeeping as an instrument "to help maintain peace and security in support of an ongoing effort at a political solution." It is made clear that CSCE peacekeeping activities will be completely in line with Article 52 of the United Nations Charter in that they will only be undertaken with the consent of the parties concerned. Somewhat surprisingly CSCE totally excluded itself taking enforcement action, even if this were to be authorized by the Security Council. It also, most importantly, stated that the CSCE was "prepared to seek, on a case-by-case basis, the support of international institutions, such as EC, NATO and WEU, as well as other institutions and mechanisms, including the peacekeeping mechanism of the CIS." This last reference to the somewhat shadowy mechanism of the Commonwealth of Independent States of the former Soviet Union was insisted on at the last moment by the Russian representative and was accepted with reluctance by many delegations.

In practice the structure of the CSCE is heavily handicapped by the fact that its decisions have to be made by consensus of the 53 members. In fact, both NATO and WEU have worked directly with the United Nations, rather than the CSCE, since July 1992 in providing elements to implement UN resolutions on the former Yugoslavia. In the margins of the CSCE July 1992 Helsinki Summit the nine WEU Foreign Ministers met and decided to send a WEU naval force to the Adriatic to monitor the effectiveness of the economic sanctions imposed by the UN Security Council on "Yugoslavia" (Serbia and Montenegro). Later the same morning they met again in the NATO Council with their seven colleagues from the other member states of NATO and agreed on the deployment of a NATO sanction-monitoring force.

NATO has subsequently made airborne early warning aircraft available to work together with French and American AWACS aircraft to monitor the application of the UN restrictions on flights over Bosnia. WEU assembled a package of forces from its member states which were submitted to the UN Secretary-General to provide the bulk of the UNPROFOR 2 force in Bosnia. Exceptionally these forces were provided to the UN at no charge to the United Nations, with all costs being carried by the countries concerned.[5] NATO provided significant elements of the mobile headquarters of its Northern Army Group to provide command and control functions for the forces supplied to UNPROFOR 2 in Bosnia. This force has been under the command of the French General Philippe Morillon, which demonstrates the flexibility of the European cooperation as France does not normally take part in the integrated command structure of NATO of which the Northern Army Group headquarters forms part.

NATO was also asked by the Secretary-General of the UN to assist in the planning for the imposition of a "no-fly zone" over Bosnia which since its introduction has been under the the the operational control of NATO's Fifth Allied Tactical Air Force based in Vicenza, Italy. It seemed highly probable that, if the Security Council had decided on an enhanced military presence in Bosnia to ensure the implementation of the Vance-Owen peace plan, NATO and its member states would have played a large part in planning and commanding it. NATO itself has already begun to examine the possibility of cooperation on peacekeeping with its NACC partners including Russia and the combined force in Bosnia could have been a first example of this.

This substantial practical development in cooperation between regional organizations and the United Nations in Europe was forced by the necessity to respond to the Yugoslav situation. It was matched at the political level by the cooperation after August 1992 between the United Nations and the European Community in the search for a political solution in former Yugoslavia, with David Owen as the representative of the European Community, and

Cyrus Vance and subsequently Thorvald Stoltenberg representing the United Nations. While the CSCE aspires, as we have seen, to be a regional arrangement under Chapter VIII of the UN Charter (Articles 52 and 53) able to resolve problems among its own members, bodies like NATO, WEU and the EC which are acting in direct cooperation with the United Nations would seem to be covered by Article 48 which speaks of the use by the members of "appropriate international agencies of which they are members" to implement the decisions of the Security Council. One could even see the planning for Bosnia in the Military Committee of NATO as an indication of how that body could become one of the "regional sub-committees" of the UN's Military Staff Committee which Article 47.4 of the Charter permits. Perhaps eventually there could be a formal agreement between WEU or NATO and the United Nations on the availability of forces on the basis mentioned in Article 43.3 of the Charter where explicit reference is made to agreements "between the Security Council and groups of members."

While the development of more effective regional security arrangements may help to ensure a timely response in the case of future European crises, it is not clear whether this model is appropriate in all regions. If it is not, do we need to guard against an asymmetry developing between Europe and the other regions of the world with Europeans becoming reluctant to contribute to security responsibilities in other regions?

C. THE NEW CHALLENGES OF WIDER ROLES

The unprecedented quantitative growth in UN peacekeeping forces has been matched, as already discussed, by significant qualitative changes in the roles and missions of these forces. Apart from the UNIFIL operation in South Lebanon (which has had more than 5,000 troops), traditional UN peacekeeping forces have normally had under 2,000 troops and the majority less than 500. On the other hand the operations decided on in the last two years have been significantly larger and often more heavily equipped. UNTAC in Cambodia has some 22,000 troops; UNOSOM 2 in Somalia, even after the withdrawal of the bulk of the US forces, is of a comparable size. Before any additional forces are deployed for the implementation of the Vance-Owen plan or the protection of safe areas, some 20,000 are deployed in the UN Protection Forces in Croatia, Bosnia and Macedonia. In

Mozambique the Security Council has agreed to deploy more than 7,000 troops to supervise the end of internal hostilities and the transition to democracy. This is more than ten times as many as were deployed in Angola and perhaps reflects the unhappy experience there.

The other important change has been the much greater participation of the forces of the Permanent Members of the Security Council in these forces. Although there was limited British and French participation in "traditional" UN peacekeeping forces in Cyprus and South Lebanon, we now have Russian troops in Croatia, more than 3,000 U.S. forces continuing in UNOSOM 2 in Somalia (where the overall UN force commander is the Turkish General Cevik Bir with an American deputy) and U.S. participation in ONUMOZ in Mozambique (under a UN force commander), as well as significant French and British forces in Bosnia, and French in Somalia. In Cambodia there is a Chinese battalion deployed for the first time. It is not surprising, given the large numbers of forces now required, that Russia and the United States are contributing, but it is of interest that in 1993 U.S. forces are coming under the command of a UN force commander who is not an American and who is answerable to the Security Council.

The increased size of the forces is some measure of the increased difficulty of the operations in which UN forces are now involved. The absence of an effective government in Somalia, the ineffectiveness of the Bosnian government's control over its own territory and the inadequacy of cease-fires have meant that the UN forces have required more muscle and authority than in traditional peacekeeping. In addition the exposure, in particular of the Somalia and former Yugoslav and Cambodian operations, to intensive media coverage has considerably complicated the tasks of the force commanders, UN Secretariat authorities, and the political and military leaders of the countries contributing forces. UN operations in the past have rarely received such publicity.

The rapid increase in the size and complexity of peacekeeping operations has opened discussions on participation in peacekeeping operations in most Trilateral countries. The specific debates, particularly in Japan and Germany, are considered in Masashi Nishihara's chapter. If, as is probable, the demand for forces expands and those participating run greater risks, there will be intense debates in all our countries as to what our responsibilities for global collective security are and how we should fulfill them.

Even if we accept that our national interests are not restricted to those cases where we have a direct interest but that all democratic countries share a long-term indirect interest in the preservation of the norms and standards of international law, there will still be very difficult questions about when it is feasible and desirable for the United Nations or its individual members to act. It will be very difficult for the international community to say that it is unable to act in a particular situation, but going into too many situations where the international organization is unsuccesful will not increase its credibility nor the long-term readiness of member states to provide forces. The decisions as to when to act and when not to will be particularly difficult in the many "grey area" conflicts now occurring which are not between formal state entities but linked to civil war or government collapse.

While few would admit that the "CNN factor" is critical, the amount of media coverage clearly affects the attention that problems elsewhere in the world receive in our legislatures. The Secretary-General of the United Nations talks wisely of the advantages of preventive diplomacy supported where appropriate by preventive deployments, in his report on *An Agenda for Peace.* This is true, but it is probably a counsel of perfection as in major modern democracies it will be difficult to persuade decision-makers to expend resources and put their armed forces at risk until a crisis has become acute. The United Nations' own resources in the Secretariat are at the moment far too limited to be effective in this field, and certainly attention should be given to strengthening them along the lines suggested by the Secretary-General in *An Agenda for Peace.*

Can we learn from the experience of all too many crises where in retrospect it is clear that a small effort expended early would have been much more effective and avoided the need for much greater effort later? The concept of deterrence (in its general non-nuclear sense) is important in many situations, and one of the lessons many would draw from our mistakes in former Yugoslavia is that our actions and statements gave the impression to the parties that military force could not ultimately be used. However nothing is more dangerous in the long term for the international community than to threaten to use force and then fail to do so irrespective of what occurs. The best way to ensure that deterrence does not fail is to have an assured and usable military response available if it does.

D. PROPOSALS FOR THE FUTURE

The rapid developments in the last two years and the developing cooperation between the United Nations and regional organizations are too recent for all the necessary conclusions as to future structures to be drawn. Some conclusions, however, are already clear. If, as seems likely, the international community and the Trilateral countries are going to face continuing demands for substantial peacekeeping forces, one clear conclusion is that arrangements to ensure the rapid deployment of peacekeeping forces should be improved.

It would be useful to consider planning for three levels of UN forces.[6] If a reality is to be made of early preventive deployment the United Nations should have at its permanent disposal a highly trained standing ready force of some four or five battalions (each of some 600-700 troops) drawn from one or two nations and trained to operate as a single operating unit. There might be a *roulement* so that over a period of time different nations would contribute forces. Such a force would be regularly exercised on its own and from time to time with the national forces designated as being available to the United Nations on call. Such a force could be used quickly for preventive deployments or as the advance guard of a more substantial force. Some have suggested that such a force should be directly recruited and serve as the United Nations' "Swiss Guards." This certainly merits consideration, although the advantages of having some of the forces coming from larger countries (with the professional training and experience this implies) probably weighs against this. The force would be funded by all the members of the United Nations.

At a second level, the United Nations should have rapid deployment forces from the armed forces of member states which could be deployed at a few days notice. Some have argued that these should be available on the basis of brigade-size groups (about 5,000 persons each) from contributing nations. This is however a very substantial commitment for many smaller UN members, and it could be that regional groups of members could cooperate to make up a force of brigade-size. If ten countries or groups of countries were each prepared to provide a brigade group, it would be possible for the UN to deploy forces of up to 50,000 men, although smaller forces could, of course, be deployed as appropriate. Such brigade groups would need to have a capacity for enforcement action and would therefore require heavier equipment than has been deployed with "traditional" peacekeeping forces. (It would not of course be necessary for these forces always to be deployed in an enforcement mode.) This change may present certain problems for some of the countries that have previously been major contributors to UN forces, providing lightly armed forces for "traditional" peacekeeping roles. It would obviously be desirable for these rapid deployment forces to have opportunities to undertake joint exercises from time to time, and for contingency arrangements for command structures and headquarters to be developed.

Such rapid deployment forces would enable the Security Council to have at its disposal forces for an early response to a conflict or potential conflict situation. The very availability of such a capacity at the disposal of the international community could have a deterrent effect.

The arrangements by which these forces would be made available to the United Nations could be under formal agreement with the Security Council as set out in Article 43 of the Charter. There would be an advantage for the countries concerned if this were done, as they would then have the right under Article 44 (if not currently a member of the Security Council) to take part in the Council's decisions whenever their forces were involved.

If there were serious aggression by a regional power, as in the case of Iraq against Kuwait, the forces described above would not suffice and it would be necessary to create a coalition of forces of an appropriate size. Whether this would have to be done ad hoc in any particular case or whether forces could be earmarked for such operations needs to be decided. The latter would clearly be preferable as this would permit the troops concerned to receive training appropriate for participation in such a UN force.

A major problem for any UN force whose size goes beyond a brigade or whose mandate goes beyond "traditional" peacekeeping has been command structures and headquarters. Countries are justifiably reluctant to make their forces available for operations that may involve combat unless they are satisfied with the command arrangements. The solution adopted in Korea, Iraq and more recently Somalia with the United States providing the lead has ensured effective command but should not be regarded as a universal solution. It is clear from the discussions in the Security Council about the command structure that would have been used if a force had been deployed into Bosnia to implement the Vance-Owen plan that there can be a conflict between military efficiency and wider aspects of political acceptability. The problems become more difficult as the size of the force and the risk of conflict increases. The deployment of elements from a NATO headquarters for the UNPROFOR 2 force in Bosnia suggests a limited multilateral alternative. NATO's experience in developing a common military culture and common multinational operating procedures is of great value when forces from its member countries need to cooperate within UN forces. In the future other regional structures may be able to contribute comparable assets.

It would clearly be desirable that the rapid deployment forces discussed above have a permanent planning staff, and contingency arrangements for headquarters which should be regularly exercised on an integrated basis. The work undertaken in NATO headquarters and in WEU's planning cell could make important contributions to this.

At the beginning of this chapter it was argued that in the future the process of crisis management and conflict resolution will have political, economic, and humanitarian dimensions as well as military dimensions. It would therefore be useful to strengthen the structures at the United Nations headquarters to assist in the non-military dimensions of crisis management and increase the civilian units to be dispatched into the field alongside military forces. On some occasions the UN may be working in cooperation with regional arrangements, but without some strengthening at the center the latter are unlikely to be able to cope with all the problems. The coordination of crisis management—of regional and United Nations bodies as well as non-governmental humanitarian agencies—is by no means easy. The situation can be particularly difficult when the intervention is in a country where government activity is totally lacking or grossly inadequate. While it would be desirable for these wider coordination mechanisms to have opportunities for advance contingency planning, it is even more difficult to arrange this than in the case of military forces, given the extensive range of agencies which could be involved. They would almost certainly vary from case to case.

NOTES

1. The Russian veto on May 12, 1993, of a proposal to rearrange the financing of UNFICYP was more related to Russia's economic situation than to political differences.
2. This distinction is broadly similar to that made between "Chapter VI action" and "Chapter VII action" although, as has been seen in former Yugoslavia, this distinction is more difficult to make in UN operations today than in the period when peacekeeping was a question of freezing a situation after a cease-fire had been established.
3. The members of WEU are Belgium, Germany, France, Italy, Luxembourg, Netherlands, Portugal, Spain and the United Kingdom. In December 1992 Greece signed a Treaty of Accession to WEU. Iceland, Norway and Turkey are becoming Associate Members, and Denmark and Ireland Observers.
4. The term "regional arrangement" was particularly appropriate for the CSCE, which is not a treaty-based organization.
5. This procedure and the problems it can produce are discussed in more detail in Enid Schoettle's chapter.
6. I am grateful to the United Nations Association of the United States of America for the October 1992 report *Partners for Peace: Strengthening Collective Security for the 21st Century*, on which I have drawn in this section. The report was prepared under the supervision of a National Advisory Committee chaired by R. James Woolsey. The project was directed by Jeffrey Laurenti.

III. FINANCING UN PEACEKEEPING

Enid C.B. Schoettle

"Will this Organization face the economic consequences of its own actions and how will it be done? Further, if it is not willing to face the financial consequences of its own decisions, is it then prepared to change its substantive policies? There is no third alternative."

Secretary-General Dag Hammarskjöld, 1960

"A chasm has developed between the tasks entrusted to this Organization and the financial means provided to it. The truth of the matter is that our vision cannot really extend to the prospect opening before us as long as our financing remains myopic."

Secretary-General Boutros Boutros-Ghali,
An Agenda for Peace, 1992

Since the end of the Cold War, the UN has entered a new chapter and become a "qualitatively different body":[1] seeking to serve as the ultimate custodian of international peace and security as its founders envisaged in 1945. Nowhere is this more apparent than in the field of peacekeeping. Rather than directly deploying their own national military forces, governments are now turning to the UN to handle most of the world's active military conflicts. Since 1988, fifteen new UN peacekeeping operations have been established: more in the past five years than the 13 peacekeeping forces established between 1948 and 1987. They have ranged across four continents: Afghanistan, the Iran/Iraq and Iraq/Kuwait borders, Cambodia, Nicaragua, El Salvador, former Yugoslavia, Namibia, Western Sahara, Angola, Somalia, and Mozambique. These new UN operations, as Roper notes, are no longer solely military in function, but have wide responsibilities for human rights monitoring, refugee assistance and repatriation, the conduct of elections and referenda, civil administration, public information programs, humanitarian assistance, and economic and social development. The number of forces have also increased dramatically: 9,666 UN troops and military observers were deployed in

1987, compared with 75,738 on May 31, 1993.[2] These UN peacekeepers come from 74 countries: 41% of the UN's membership.

The UN's expanding role in helping the world contain conflicts has earned high-level endorsement from most member states. In January 1992 the UN Security Council met for the first time since 1945 at the summit level, and the fifteen heads of state and government announced:

> The members of the Council stress the importance of strengthening and improving the United Nations to increase its effectiveness. They are determined to assume fully their responsibilities within the United Nations Organization in the framework of the Charter.[3]

In July 1992 at their Munich Summit, the leaders of the G-7 also pledged the United Nations their support:

> The new challenges underlie the need for strengthening the UN....The Secretary General's report "An Agenda for Peace" is a valuable contribution to the work of the United Nations on preventive diplomacy, peace-making and peace-keeping. We assure him of our readiness to provide the political support and resources needed to maintain international peace and security.[4]

TABLE 1

Top 15 Contributors to the 1992 Regular and Peacekeeping Budgets of the UN

	Regular Budget			Peacekeeping Budgets	
1.	United States	25.0%	1.	United States	31.7%
2.	Japan	12.5%	2.	Japan	12.5%
3.	Germany	8.9%	3.	Germany	8.9%
4.	Russia*	6.7%	4.	Russia*	8.5%
5.	France	6.0%	5.	France	7.6%
6.	United Kingdom	5.0%	6.	United Kingdom	6.4%
7.	Italy	4.3%	7.	Italy	4.3%
8.	Canada	3.1%	8.	Canada	3.1%
9.	Spain	2.0%	9.	Spain	2.0%
10.	Ukraine*	1.9%	10.	Ukraine*	1.9%
11.	Brazil*	1.6%	11.	Australia*	1.5%
12.	Australia*	1.5%	12.	Netherlands	1.5%
13.	Netherlands	1.5%	13.	Sweden	1.1%
14.	Sweden	1.1%	14.	Belgium	1.1%
15.	Belgium	1.1%	15.	China*	1.0%
	Total	**82.2%**			**93.1%**

Source: Secretariat Document ST/ADM/SER. B/397 of March 18, 1993, *Assessment of Member States' Contributions for the Financing of the United Nations Protection Force (UNPROFOR) from 12 January 1992 to 20 February 1993.*

* non-Trilateral countries

Despite these ringing endorsements, one thing that has not kept pace with the changes since 1987 is the UN's resource base. A continuing financial crisis is paralyzing the UN's ability to carry out its rapidly expanding activities. This is not a new phenomenon, but unless the UN's financial problems are resolved and more reliable financial mechanisms put in place, the organization will not be able to play the new role which governments—and particularly the Trilateral governments—claim they want it to play. Finding the financial and material resources to do its job is now the key problem facing the UN.

Solving the financial problems of the United Nations is the responsibility of all its members. The United Nations is an inter-governmental organization of sovereign states and "what it can do depends on the common ground that they create between them."[5] Practically speaking however, such solutions are the special responsibility of the industrialized states, particularly the Trilateral countries. Table 1 shows that the top 15 contributors provide the bulk of UN funding. To drive the point home, Table 2 shows that the current Trilateral countries carry a comparable share.

TABLE 2
**Current Trilateral Commission Countries,
1992 Assessed Contributions to the Regular and Peacekeeping Budgets**

	Regular Budget	Peacekeeping Budgets
United States	25.00%	31.74%
Japan	12.45%	12.45%
Germany	8.93%	8.93%
France	6.00%	7.62%
United Kingdom	5.02%	6.37%
Italy	4.29%	4.29%
Canada	3.11%	3.11%
Spain	1.98%	1.98%
Netherlands	1.50%	1.50%
Sweden	1.11%	1.11%
Belgium	1.06%	1.06%
Austria	0.75%	0.75%
Denmark	0.65%	0.65%
Norway	0.55%	0.55%
Portugal	0.20%	0.04%
Ireland	0.18%	0.18%
Trilateral Total	**72.78%**	**82.33%**
Other 165 UN members	27.22%	17.67%

Source: Same as for Table 1

Certain Trilateral countries have been exemplary in meeting their financial obligations to the United Nations, as well as supporting the United Nations in other ways. If all Trilateral governments made a concerted effort to strengthen both the UN's financial condition and their own national policies on UN financing, the UN's problems would be largely solved.

An essential prerequisite to resolving the UN's financial problems is to keep them in realistic perspective. Even in these years of rapidly increasing demand for UN peacekeeping, the costs are miniscule compared to national defense establishments or other national government activities. The UN's regular assessed budget in 1992 was $1.14 billion, just about the size of the budget of New York City's Fire Department. 1992 expenditures on UN peacekeeping operations were $1.37 billion—less than New York City's Police Department budget. The combined UN expenditures for both the regular budget and peacekeeping in 1992 were less than the cost of three Stealth bombers (at $1 billion a unit) or two days of Desert Storm (at $1.5 billion per day).

Governments have always made substantial additional voluntary contributions to support UN peacekeeping operations, and such contributions are increasing. But the total voluntary contributions to the operations in Cambodia, Somalia and former Yugoslavia add up to no more than the costs of three or four more Stealth bombers or two or three more days of Desert Storm.

The trend is clear. Peacekeeping—which now involves not only "traditional" peacekeeping but also more robust peace-enforcement and a widening range of police, political, humanitarian and social-economic functions—is a rapidly growing activity. Costs increased five-fold between 1988 and 1992. Over the course of 1993, the costs of UN peacekeeping are projected to triple again. This is a very dynamic rate of growth at a time of declining defense and international affairs budgets in Trilateral countries, but it is well within the range that governments ordinarily consider normal defense expenditures. Trilateral governments will need to recognize that UN peacekeeping is now a central, ongoing mission for their national security, and be prepared to fund it accordingly.

This paper is divided into three sections. The first describes current methods of financing UN peacekeeping. The second describes current problems in financing UN peacekeeping. The final section makes two types of recommendations: (a) policies for Trilateral governments and the regional organizations to which they belong; and (b) policies which governments should urge on the UN.

A. CURRENT METHODS OF FINANCING U.N. PEACEKEEPING

There are three categories of UN financing: mandatory assessed contributions to the regular budget; separate mandatory assessed contributions to individual peacekeeping operations; and voluntary contributions of various kinds.

Figure 1 indicates how the relative shares of these resources have shifted over the past decade. The annual cost of peacekeeping now substantially exceeds the regular budget. In recent years, total voluntary contributions to UN programs and activities linked to the regular budget have also exceeded the regular budget.[6] The regular budget and voluntary contributions, while formally distinct from the mechanisms for funding peacekeeping, underpin and complement peacekeeping financing in important ways. In addition, four types of UN financial reserves—including a Peacekeeping Reserve Fund established in 1992—can also be drawn on to support peacekeeping. A brief description of these UN financial mechanisms is in an appendix at the back of this chapter.

Since 1962, the cost of peacekeeping per se has been considered a mandatory expense of the United Nations, subject to the principle of collective financial responsibility. This was confirmed after the USSR, France, and several other states refused to pay their assessments for peacekeeping operations dispatched to Egypt in 1956 and the Congo in 1960.[7] In 1962, an advisory opinion from the International Court of Justice found that Article 17 of the UN Charter, which holds that all expenditures appropriated by the General Assembly are to be borne by all member states, pertained to expenditures for peacekeeping.

Since 1956, peacekeeping has also been financed outside the regular budget through a separate assessment for each operation. This is justified on the grounds that peacekeeping costs are unpredictable and thus not easily accommodated in advance within the regular budget. As a result, whenever the Security Council authorizes a new peacekeeping operation, the General Assembly must approve a new assessment before it can be fully deployed.

The current special assessment formula for peacekeeping was instituted in 1973,[8] and divides member states into four categories. The "economically least developed states" pay 10% of their assessment rate for the regular budget, and the "economically less developed states" pay 20%. The industrialized countries pay the same assessment rate as for the regular budget. The five Permanent Members of the Security Council pay the remainder, or approximately

FIGURE 1
Growth in Biennial UN Expenditures, 1982-1993
(in millions of U.S. dollars)

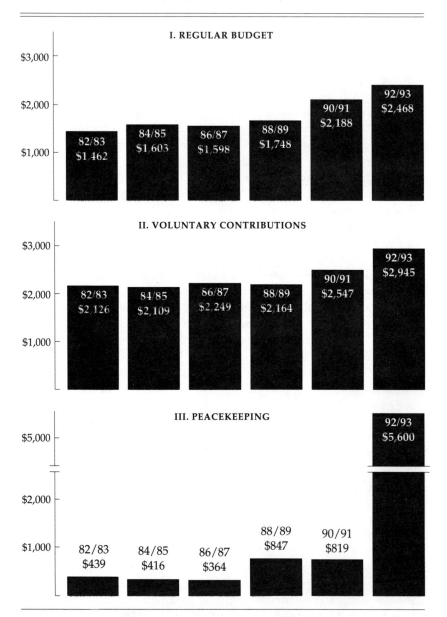

Source: Adapted from Independent Advisory Group, "Financing an Effective United Nations: Report of the Independent Advisory Group on U.N. Financing" (New York: The Ford Foundation, February 1993), p.30.

22% above their regular assessment rates. In 1992, this meant that the Permanent Members paid 56% of the entire peacekeeping assessment. While retaining the principle of collective financial responsibility, the formula both minimizes the burden on developing countries, and recognizes the special responsibilities of the five Permanent Members and their special privilege of the veto.

Eleven of the current thirteen peacekeeping operations are funded by special peacekeeping assessments. The Truce Supervision Organization in the Middle East (established in 1948) and the Military Observer Group in India and Pakistan (established in 1949) continue to be funded in the regular UN budget, since no procedure for special peacekeeping assessments existed at the time they were established. The Peace-keeping Force in Cyprus, established in 1964, was funded by voluntary contributions until the Security Council decision to change its financing to an assessed basis effective June 1, 1993.[9] The 1992 costs and projected 1993 estimates for current operations are listed in Table 3.

The major cause of the UN's current financial crisis is delayed payment or non-payment of assessments. This results in periodic cash flow crises and the depletion of available reserves.

States are required to pay their assessments on or about January 31 in a given calendar year for the regular budget and thirty days after receiving a peacekeeping assessment. In fact, very few countries consistently pay their assessments on time and in full. In 1993, only 15 countries (out of 180) paid their regular assessment by the January 31 due date, providing less than 11% of the regular budget.[10] The UN's only weapon against this practice is Article 19 which provides that a member state may lose its vote in the General Assembly if its arrears equal its total assessments over the preceding two years. Now in effect against South Africa and a few small states, Article 19 has clearly not deterred late payments.

States pay assessments late or not at all for various reasons. One is national budget cycles. For example, in 1981, the United States, the UN's largest contributor, decided to slip one fiscal year in appropriating its regular assessments. Rather than paying the assessment quarterly throughout the fiscal year in which it fell due, as had been U.S. practice until 1981, the Reagan Administration began to authorize assessments in the subsequent fiscal year beginning in October: that is, in the fourth quarter of the UN's financial year. This U.S. practice puts the UN in a financial choke collar for three-quarters of each year. Japan, now the UN's second largest contributor,

TABLE 3
Current Peacekeeping Missions,
Assessments and Estimated Expenditures

Mission	Authorization: Assessment	1992 Cost	Projected 1993
UNTSO (Middle East)	Authorized in the Regular Budget	$25 million	$31 million
UNMOGIP (India/Pakistan)	Authorized in the Regular Budget	$6 million	$7 million
UNFYCIP (Cyprus)	Voluntary Contributions until June 1993	$31 million	$17 million
ONUCA (Nicaragua)	11/91 - 4/92: $12 million	$7 million	N/A
UNDOF (Middle East)	12/92 - 5/93: $17 million	$39 million	$36 million
UNIFIL (Lebanon)	2/93 - 7/93: $74 million	$153 million	$146 million
UNIKOM (Iraq-Kuwait)	5/93 - 10/93: $19 million	$68 million	$65 million
UNAVEM II (Angola)	11/92 - 2/93: $25 million	$67 million	$36 million
ONUSAL (El Salvador)	12/92 - 5/93: $12 million	$35 million	$34 million
MINURSO (Western Sahara)	Authorized 9/91; not yet fully operational	$18 million	$35 million
UNPROFOR (ex-Yugoslavia)	10/92 - 6/93: $466 million	$222 million	$1.02 billion
UNAMIC (Cambodia advance mission)	11/91 - 4/92: $33 million	$20 million	N/A
UNTAC (Cambodia)	11/92 - 7/93: $548 million	$637 million	$1 billion
UNOSOM I (Somalia)	5/92 - 4/93: $108 million	$39 million	N/A
UNOSOM II (Somalia)	5/93 - 6/93: $300 million	N/A	$1.5 billion
ONUMOZ (Mozambique)	10/92 - 6/93: $140 million	N/A	$210 million
TOTAL		**$1.4 billion**	**$4.2 billion**

Source: Adapted from Independent Advisory Group, "Financing an Effective United Nations: Report of the Independent Advisory Group on U.N. Financing" (New York: The Ford Foundation, February 1993), p. 29. See also *Background Note, United Nations Peace-keeping Operations*, PS/DPI/15/Rev. 4 (United Nations, May 1993) and ST/ADM/SER.B/411 of June 8, 1993 (Status of Contributions as at May 31, 1993).

generally pays its assessment beginning in late spring, after the Diet appropriates the funds. Germany, the fourth largest contributor, pays half of its assessment in January, the other half in June.

Certain states also withhold payments on policy grounds. Beginning in 1979, the United States, followed by other industrialized countries, began selectively withholding a portion of their assessments for items deemed inimical to their interests: for example, programs benefitting the Palestine Liberation Organization (PLO) and the Law of the Sea Preparatory Commission. Most serious, pursuant to the Kassebaum-Solomon Amendment to the Foreign Relations Authorization Act of 1985, between 1986 and 1989 the U.S. unilaterally withheld 20% of its assessment for the regular budget each year, in order to press the UN to adopt major reforms in budgetary and administrative practices. This produced a major financial crisis at the UN. It was largely as a result of this pressure that consensus budgeting, zero real growth in the regular budget, and certain reductions in Secretariat personnel were brought about.

After these reforms were put into place, in 1991 the United States began to repay $220 million in arrears for the regular budget and $157 million in arrears for peacekeeping over a five-year period.[11] It is likely never to repay an amount of approximately $115 million to the regular budget for specific policy withholdings, many of which are mandated by the Congress. However defensible these policy objectives may be, both selective and across-the-board withholdings are a breach of a UN member's legal obligation to pay assessed contributions in full.

A third reason for late payment is economic crisis. Beginning in mid-1991, the then Soviet Union, the UN's third largest contributor, began falling behind in its payments both to the regular budget and to peacekeeping. Economic problems are likely to continue in Russia, as well as in the other republics of the former Soviet Union, resulting in continuing delayed payments. A number of developing countries also have grave difficulties in keeping current on their assessments.

For all these reasons, since the onset of the UN financial crisis in the mid-1980s, unpaid assessments to the United Nations have increased. As of May 31, 1993, $924 million was owed the regular budget. 133 countries—three-fourths of the UN's members—owed assessments due in 1993 or earlier.[12] Two countries, however, accounted for fully 66%: the U.S. owed $518 million (56%), and Russia $91 million (10%) of all outstanding assessments for the regular budget.

As of May 31, 1993, outstanding assessments for peacekeeping totalled $1.28 billion. The United States owed $314 million (25%) and

Russia owed $410 million (31%) of all outstanding peacekeeping assessments. Since the five Permanent Members of the Security Council now provide 55% of the total costs of peacekeeping, their payments are critical if peacekeeping operations are to remain solvent.[13]

These growing arrears have forced the UN to deplete its reserve funds to meet current operating requirements. Once reserves are exhausted, the UN must then resort to borrowing from the few peacekeeping operations with surplus cash, in order to pay salaries and other regular budget obligations and to support other peacekeeping operations. The situation is not improving. For the first time in its history, the UN entered 1993 with its regular budget in debt to current peacekeeping operations. In short, the UN is broke.

B. CURRENT PROBLEMS IN FINANCING U.N. PEACEKEEPING

Having increased five-fold since 1988, peacekeeping costs reached an all-time high of $1.37 billion in 1992. The UN projects much higher peacekeeping costs in 1993. This 1993 estimate of $4.2 billion includes only the projected costs mandated as of May 31, 1993. If, as is possible, the mandates of missions in Cambodia, former Yugoslavia and/or Somalia are further expanded, the 1993 cost of peacekeeping will exceed $4.2 billion. Moreover, if new peacekeeping operations were to be deployed in crisis areas such as Georgia, Haiti, Liberia, Sudan, Tajikistan, or Zaire, the costs will go higher still.

If the required resources are to be raised, the system for financing UN peacekeeping must be revised, and soon. Four issues need to be addressed:

- The UN financial crisis and peacekeeping.
- The difficulty of predicting peacekeeping costs.
- Anomalies in the special scale of assessments.
- Voluntary funding and collective financial responsibility.

1. The UN Financial Crisis and Peacekeeping

The UN is often required to send peacekeeping troops at short notice to an area of conflict. Expenses often need to be met very quickly, before member states can be assessed. The up-front costs of transporting troops and equipment are high, and the greater the urgency, the greater the need for expensive airlift. The UN must purchase or lease the equipment and services which are not provided by the troop contingents.

In principle, UN reserves should meet these initial expenses. But, as noted above, since the mid-1980s reserves have been often depleted. The new Peacekeeping Reserve Fund, while a useful initiative, has only $59 million of its authorized $150 million in hand, which amounts to a little over 1% of *currently* projected 1993 peacekeeping costs.

With shortfalls in the payment of peacekeeping assessments and depleted reserves, the UN is forced to raise cash from two sources.[14] First, the UN frequently delays reimbursing states that provide troop contingents and equipment. It currently owes over $200 million to troop-contributing countries.[15] Some countries have not been paid for years: troop contributors to UNIFIL in Lebanon, for example, have not been repaid for costs incurred in 1988. Many traditional troop contributors are owed money for several operations. Their sense of exploitation by the "system" of financing peacekeeping and particularly by those who fail to pay their assessments is increasing, and understandably so.[16]

Second, as noted above, the UN frequently must use balances in certain peacekeeping accounts to cover shortfalls in the regular budget or other peacekeeping accounts, or to fund the start-up of new peacekeeping operations. Given the high costs of several new peacekeeping operations, however, shortfalls in assessed payments for them could easily exhaust whatever cash is available in all other peacekeeping accounts. At that point, the regular budget and all of the peacekeeping operations could run out of money at once.[17]

The UN's financial crisis also hamstrings its ability to support peacekeeping operations in other ways. The regular budget covers the costs of running the Department of Peacekeeping Operations itself; the Department of Political Affairs, which negotiates the settlements which peacekeeping operations then implement; and the wide range of central administrative, personnel, financial, legal and logistical functions which support peacekeeping operations.[18] Because zero real growth budgeting has been applied to the regular budget since 1986, those units which support the Department of Peacekeeping Operations have been under increasing pressure. As only one example, there are now forty budget officers in the Controller's office working on the regular budget but only twelve assigned to peacekeeping budgets: at a time when the total costs of peacekeeping far exceed the regular budget.

2. The Difficulty of Predicting Peacekeeping Costs

The emergency nature of most peacekeeping operations makes them hard to predict in advance and thus hard to accommodate in both UN and national budget cycles. Each peacekeeping operation is separately funded with its own account. States receive separate assessments for each mission whenever the mandate period is renewed. Since most of the thirteen current missions are established for six-month periods from the date the Security Council first authorized them, Treasury Departments typically receive two letters per mission per year, throughout the year.[19] At a time of rapidly escalating costs for peacekeeping, states find it increasingly difficult to accommodate these frequent and somewhat unpredictable assessments within national budgets. As a result, on average, only 36% of peacekeeping assessments are paid within three months after assessments are issued.[20]

The budgetary process within the UN is also cumbersome. When a peacekeeping operation is approved by the Security Council, the budget is then drawn up in two different offices: the Field Operations Division, and the Office of Programme Planning, Budget and Finance. The budget is then submitted to the Advisory Committee on Administrative and Budgetary Questions (ACABQ), the Fifth Committee of the General Assembly, and finally to the General Assembly for approval by consensus. Only then can letters of assessment be dispatched to governments. Meanwhile, before a budget is passed, under the Secretary-General's spending authority for unforeseen and extraordinary circumstances, the Secretariat can contract for necessary equipment and services only up to $3 million per mission, or, if the ACABQ has acted, up to $10 million.[21]

This complex process of peacekeeping budgeting is time-consuming, micro-managed, and often contentious. In recent years it has entailed weeks or indeed months of argument about necessary expenditures.[22] The Security Council wants more budget information early in its consideration of a new mission, but the Secretariat is loath to provide detailed estimates, out of fear that the Permanent Members and other major contributors will pare the mission.

The problems associated with the somewhat tentative nature of the Secretariat's early budget projections are exacerbated by the minimal resources expended on internal and external auditing of peacekeeping operations. The Joint Inspection Unit has only a few full- time staff working on peacekeeping operations. In the $1.6 billion budget for UNTAC in Cambodia, only $120 thousand was allocated for external auditing.[23] In the $208 million budget for UNOSOM I in Somalia, only $12 thousand was allocated for external auditing.[24] Major contributors believe fraud exists in various peacekeeping operations. They argue that they would be more willing to provide up-front funding for peacekeeping if they could be assured there would be serious auditing of the operations after the fact.

Meanwhile, for its part, the General Assembly strongly resents Security Council intrusion into its clear prerogative for budget decisions. Already alarmed by what they see as the growing power of the Security Council, leading states in the General Assembly insist on their rights to determine peacekeeping budgets. Given the inevitably somewhat sketchy nature of the Secretariat's early estimates, the subsequent highly detailed oversight by various General Assembly budget committees frequently identifies mistaken assumptions and calculations. This merely worsens the suspicions of the major contributors.

Delays in reaching agreement on budgets at the outset of peacekeeping operations in Cambodia and Yugoslavia in 1992 ran real risks of aborting these operations at their outset. In these cases, early partial appropriations were made: $200 million for UNTAC in Cambodia and $250 million for UNPROFOR in former Yugoslavia. These proved to be the only way to provide the necessary resources up front, and constitute useful precedents for the future.[25]

Apart from the complexity and institutional rivalries of the UN budget process, the costs of peacekeeping are, by their very nature, hard to predict. First, information is hard to collect. In Cambodia, for example, early reconnoitering missions could not enter Khmer Rouge areas to assess conditions and initial judgments about the need to build prefabricated housing proved wrong. Second, it is hard to answer the question: how much is enough? Peacekeeping forces operate in unpredictable situations and try to avoid the use of force. In order to protect the troops, UN planners prefer to raise higher budgets than may be required and return the funds later. Member states, however, strongly object. The tension is to some degree inevitable. Third, because of its dire financial situation, the UN Secretariat has a clear stake in budgeting at the high range of expected costs. This understandable but bad practice generates suspicion on the part of the major contributors that the UN systematically overestimates peacekeeping budgets. Finally, for political reasons, the Security Council often establishes mandates which *underestimate* the capabilities, length of time and costs required to bring a peaceful resolution to a conflict. This leads to attempts by governments to do peacekeeping "on the cheap": both courting failure and giving the impression that the UN is not up to the task.

3. Anomalies in the Special Scale of Assessments

Since its design in 1973, certain anomalies have developed in the special peacekeeping scale of assessment. They are of increased concern to many countries as the costs of peacekeeping rise. Some "economically developed" states in the former Soviet Union and Central Europe pay the same assessment rate as they do for the regular budget, despite severe economic declines. Conversely, several "economically less developed" states, including the Arab oil-exporting states and Asian "tigers," pay only 20% of their assessed rate for the regular budget, despite their relative economic strength.[26]

The 1973 assessment represented a "delicate political compromise"[27] and will be hard to change. As the total costs of peacekeeping operations rise, however, a number of countries are complaining, and the current debate in the General Assembly over how it might be changed is intense.[28] There is also a growing belief among the five Permanent Members—particularly in the U.S. Congress—that their higher levels of assessment for peacekeeping should be reconsidered, now that peacekeeping has become a central, continuing feature of the United Nations. This question of appropriate burden-sharing for peacekeeping must be addressed if the system is to be seen as legitimate and equitable.

4. Voluntary Funding and Collective Financial Responsibility

In confirming collective financial responsibility for peacekeeping, the General Assembly ratified the principle that all countries—powerful or small, rich or poor—must share in global efforts to keep the peace. The principle holds that peacekeeping operations, if supported by all countries of the world, will be seen as legitimate, credible, and even-handed, rather than as arbitrary actions dependent on the will of one or two rich powers.

It has, however, also been long-standing UN practice to solicit voluntary contributions for peacekeeping operations. Troop contributors from industrialized countries in effect donate a large share of their contingents' costs, since the UN reimbursement rate, even when repaid, does not cover their deployment costs. The United States has contributed international air and sea lift to transport UN peacekeeping forces to operations in the Congo, Suez and Somalia. Switzerland, not even a UN member, often contributes air-medical evacuation services to UN peacekeeping operations, mostly recently in Angola, Cambodia and former Yugoslavia. Over the past two decades, however, most peacekeeping costs have been raised through mandatory assessed contributions.

Three factors are now challenging this established principle. First, as peacekeeping operations increase in number and incorporate a wide variety of non-military tasks, the distinction between what have traditionally been considered the "core" activities subject to assessed contributions and the "non-core" humanitarian or economic activities supported by voluntary contributions has become blurred. Monitoring and conducting elections, and repatriating prospective voters in Namibia and the Western Sahara, for example, were so intrinsic to the political settlements which the peacekeeping operations were designed to ensure that these activities were charged to collective assessment. Some infrastructure costs in Namibia, Cambodia and Somalia, such as road repair, were also covered by mandatory assessments, because they were necessary preconditions to UN military operations in those countries.

Humanitarian and economic programs are now being negotiated as integral parts of overall peace settlements and there is no obvious limit to the potentially very large costs of such activities that can be linked to peacekeeping, particularly in countries where social and economic structures are near collapse.[29] Since UN humanitarian assistance and economic development have traditionally been funded through voluntary contributions, this pattern by and large continues, despite the exceptions noted above. In Cambodia, Japan has made substantial contributions for refugee repatriation and resettlement and for economic reconstruction. In El Salvador, the United States and Spain are the principal funders of the new criminal justice institutions and the extensive land reform programs which are central elements of the UN-sponsored peace settlement. Many Western donors are voluntarily supporting the massive programs of humanitarian assistance being carried out in former Yugoslavia and in Somalia.

Future peacekeeping operations may well founder if these necessary elements do not attract voluntary contributions. Indeed, all these non-military elements might logically be considered the collective financial responsibility of the UN, despite the obvious anomalies of, say, Mozambique being assessed for humanitarian assistance in former Yugoslavia, and vice versa. The costs are very high, however, and practicality suggests that the bulk of such funding will continue to be voluntary. Close linkages should be maintained between the Peacekeeping Operations Department and the UN humanitarian and economic development agencies, so that these components of what Secretary-General Boutros-Ghali has called "peace-building" are not dependent on the special interest and generosity of one or two wealthy states.

Second, an even more problematic challenge to the principle of collective financial responsibility is the voluntary funding of military peacekeeping units by states or regional organizations. In the September 1992 expansion of UNPROFOR into Bosnia and Herzegovina, funding of the enlarged force was provided by the states contributing additional military personnel: notably the United Kingdom, France, the Netherlands, Belgium and Spain.[30] NATO also contributed a headquarters communications unit and an AWACS monitoring force, supported in part by the common NATO infrastructure fund. These large, voluntary contributions were seen as the only way to deploy expensive and well-armed forces quickly at a time when the UN was overextended. The United States in particular viewed it as a way to shift the financial burden in former Yugoslavia to wealthy European countries with a special stake in the region. This arrangement, however, directly challenged the UN practice of treating the core costs of peacekeeping as a regular expense of the organization. At the time, a number of UN officials and governments such as Canada feared it would begin to erode the hard-won principle of collective financial responsibility for peacekeeping.[31]

This arrangement also created various operational difficulties for UNPROFOR. The financial responsibility for military observers and headquarters personnel in Bosnia and Herzegovina was unclear and caused delay and confusion. Interoperability was reduced and command and control was blurred. NATO reporting to the UN on the status of the no-fly zone was intermittent. A real risk arose that "he who pays the piper is calling the tune," despite the fact that all of UNPROFOR is clearly under UN command.

In February 1993, when recommending a short extension of UNPROFOR's mandate, Secretary-General Boutros-Ghali reversed his position of September, stating that "...this arrangement compromised the principle...that peace-keeping operations are collective activities of the United Nations...". He concluded that "...all activities of UNPROFOR in the former Yugoslavia [should] be financed in the normal manner, i.e. by assessments on the peace-keeping scale..."[32] The Security Council approved the Secretary General's recommendation when it renewed UNPROFOR's mandate in March 1993.[33] But this issue of voluntary funding of peacekeeping operations by interested states or regional organizations may well arise in the future.

A final issue concerning the links between assessed and voluntary contributions relates to UN-authorized peace enforcement. In Korea, Iraq, and recently Somalia, enforcement operations have been financed by voluntary contributions. Very large enforcement actions, such as Desert Storm, may always need to be financed in this ad hoc manner. However, as elements of peace enforcement and humanitarian intervention merge with more robust UN peacekeeping, it will be harder to keep these funding distinctions clear. The traditional distinction has already led to the perverse outcome that the United States was $314 million in arrears for UN peacekeeping operations as of May 31, 1993, while at the same time having spent approximately $750 million on the Unified Task Force (UNITAF)—the U.S.-led enforcement operation in Somalia from December 9, 1992 to April 30, 1993—before it reverted to UNOSOM II, a formal UN peacekeeping operation, on May 1, 1993.

In short, the costs of peacekeeping operations as traditionally set out in UN peacekeeping budgets bear less and less relation to the true costs of UN peacekeeping, broadly defined. A clearer identification of costs and new principles for meeting them are required if the hard-won principle of collective financial responsibility—and the credibility, legitimacy and non-discrimination which it imparts to UN peacekeeping efforts—is not to be lost.

C. POLICY RECOMMENDATIONS

Governments—above all, Trilateral governments and the regional organizations to which they belong—have it within their power to resolve the financial problems now plaguing UN peacekeeping. Resources can be made available to the United Nations in many forms: assessed financial contributions, voluntary contributions, pledges of standby military forces, pledges of non-military capabilities, and reformed procedures. If states can make such resources available to the UN reliably and efficiently, the organization will need fewer financial reserves and standing capabilities of its own.

UN peacekeeping is an accordion. If the UN is to respond to emergency situations, it must provide a sturdy frame for the instrument: the institutional and financial capacity to mobilize a response. Governments and regional organizations provide the tough but flexible bellows of the instrument—contributing the money, men and material required for a rapidly expanding response. Together they make the music.

The first half of this final section recommends policies which Trilateral governments and the regional organizations to which they belong can adopt. As Nishihara stresses, not all Trilateral governments are in a position to adopt the same policies. However, a wide array of resources are needed for peacekeeping, broadly defined: traditional peacekeeping contingents, humanitarian and other non-military assistance, and peace-enforcement capabilities. Thus, all Trilateral governments can move in complementary ways in the same direction.

The second half of this section recommends policies which Trilateral governments should encourage the UN to adopt. As Otunnu stresses, the industrial countries' policies at the UN must be seen to be legitimate by the wider membership. Moreover, many developing countries have useful resources to contribute, including troops. But there is now wide recognition in the UN that the legitimate interests of the major financial contributors—protected by the now-established tradition of consensus budgeting—are to be respected. If the Trilateral countries can converge upon solutions to the UN's problems for financing peacekeeping, those problems can be solved.

1. Policy Recommendations for Trilateral Governments and their Regional Organizations

a. Make timely payment of UN assessments and arrears.
At the moment, it is clear that the UN is not so much under-budgeted as it is under-financed. Therefore, the single greatest contribution to solving the UN's problems in financing peacekeeping would be for governments to pay their assessments in full and on time: both for the regular budget and for peacekeeping budgets. They should also pay outstanding arrears promptly.

Whatever policy issues are at stake, the stark fact is that these are legally binding obligations. It is illegal for countries to withhold assessments for reasons of policy. It is illegal to withhold assessments until the final day of the year in order to insure that the UN adopts a zero real growth budget. It is illegal to pay arrears in installments.

Above all, this is a challenge for the United States. In the past, these U.S. practices reflected a measure of collusion between the Administration and certain members of Congress. With a new

Administration now in office, this could change. It may be politically necessary to "grandfather in" some of the previous withholdings on specific policy grounds, but the practice itself should cease. Trilateral allies should stress to the U.S. government the urgent importance of these issues.

In addition, those governments whose fiscal years are out of step with the UN fiscal year should conform their appropriations cycles to meet their treaty obligations to the UN. This may require appropriating UN assessments in the previous fiscal year. Such a shift might be phased in over several years if needed.[34]

Once current assessments and arrears are paid, UN reserves will be replenished, thus relieving the financial pressure on the UN. Governments will then need to determine whether the UN requires additional reserves to meet the rising demand for peacekeeping (see Recommendation 2.a. below).

b. Shift expenditure responsibility for UN peacekeeping.

In *Agenda for Peace*, the Secretary-General suggested shifting the costs of peacekeeping into Ministries of Defense (MOD).[35] This would presumably do two things: highlight international peacekeeping as a central national security mission in the post-Cold War period; and provide access to much larger resources than typically exist in the budgets of Ministries of Foreign Affairs (MFA). In general it is true that the rising costs of peacekeeping loom huge within an MFA budget and seem much more manageable within an MOD budget. Thus it is assumed that it would relieve the financial pressures on the UN if major governments could pay their assessments for UN peacekeeping from their defense budgets.

Is this true? In practice, there is likely to be no universal prescription, and the best place for expenditure responsibility for UN peacekeeping will undoubtedly vary among different governments. Currently, only the Netherlands funds UN peacekeeping entirely from its defense budget. Several countries fund the cost of their own military participation in UN peacekeeping operations from defense budgets.

In the United States there are now difficulties in arranging for the Department of State to reimburse the Department of Defense for in-kind contributions to UN peacekeeping which count towards the U.S. assessed contribution. Shifting resources to the DOD to cover such in-kind contributions would solve this problem. However, if the DOD were to be given responsibility for paying all peacekeeping assessments, not only for U.S. participation in peacekeeping, it would be crucial for the Department of State to maintain close policy oversight. And the DOD would be understandably resistant to such a shift unless it were assured that, at a time of substantial cuts in its own budget, the new responsibility for peacekeeping would be covered by new money.

In other countries, the solution may be very different. Japan's operations in Cambodia are financed out of the Prime Minister's special reserve fund. This is a rather flexible instrument which can, for example, fund additional troops for a peacekeeping mission. If paid through the Self-Defense Agency, such an increase might be more difficult. Some European countries may also not wish to lodge the funding of UN peacekeeping fully within their Ministries of Defense.

There is much to be said for a peacekeeping contingency fund coordinated at the Presidential or Prime-Ministerial level, similar to Canada's envelope funding mechanism. This would provide funds for the MFA to pay the assessments, the MOD to pay for military participation in peacekeeping, and the Overseas Development Ministry to make non-military, humanitarian and economic contributions. This would also enable a government to calculate the total costs of and coordinate its overall policy towards UN peacekeeping.

c. Establish extensive national standby capacities.
In following up on his *Agenda for Peace* report, the Secretary-General is requesting governments to earmark standby capabilities of all sorts for rapid assignment to the UN. The in-kind contributions being solicited include not only troops but also stockpiles of necessary equipment, training, air and sea-lift, logistics, communications, and other specialized military services. The UN is conducting an extensive survey this year of the kinds of contributions governments are willing to make. It will then list these in a catalogue from which it can subsequently generate a mixed force quickly.

Thus, now is the time for national governments to respond to the UN's request for additional resources. Obviously national responses will differ, particularly in the matter of whether to proceed with a special agreement under Article 43 of the Charter or whether to make more ad hoc arrangements. Some Trilateral countries have already designated particular standby units on call to the UN. The United States wants to respond with a different approach: not stating in advance what it will earmark for the UN, but waiting to learn from the UN what the United States could best contribute. Either approach should be useful to the UN, as long as the arrangements constitute serious political commitments.

Much can also be done by governments to assist in the planning and management of UN peacekeeping operations. By enlarging the political-military staffs in their national missions in New York, Trilateral countries could make more on-the-spot inputs into early planning for peacekeeping operations. Seconding more military officers to UN headquarters to help in such planning would also be a major contribution. For example, the UN Field Operations Division now has twenty staff to plan all the logistics for all UN peacekeeping operations: from berets to beans to bullets. Appropriate military specialists contributed by governments would be very welcome.

Money also can be appropriated by national governments and held in reserve for UN peacekeeping assessments. A model is the International Peacekeeping Act of 1992, by which the U.S. Congress authorized $700 million for the payment of future assessments to unspecified UN peacekeeping operations. It was through this mechanism that the United States was able to pay its mounting peacekeeping assessments promptly in 1992. If all major contributors had such contingency funds, the response to UN assessment requests could be much more rapid.

Finally, as Roper has discussed, regional organizations can provide standby capacities to the UN. NATO and WEU have much to contribute to UN peacekeeping operations in the form of integrated units and standardized procedures, as they are likely to do if there is an expansion of UNPROFOR in Bosnia and Herzegovina to implement a peace settlement. Regional organizations elsewhere in the world are only beginning to contemplate combined military structures, but skeletal arrangements can be encouraged.

d. Maintain collective responsibility with voluntary contributions.
There are those who believe the time has come to rethink the principle of collective financial responsibility for UN peacekeeping. They argue that at a time of much incipient conflict in the world, countries should support the resolution of those conflicts in which they have particular interests. Such a departure would, however, undermine the international consensus that it is everyone's responsibility and in everyone's interest to maintain the peace. It is this consensus, after all, which gives the resolutions of the Security Council political legitimacy and weight. It is thus politically

important that even the poorest countries of the world contribute to UN peacekeeping operations, even if the 1992 peacekeeping assessments for, say Chad, were only $15 thousand as compared to $191 million for Japan.[36]

Moreover, a departure from the principle of collective responsibility would create two unequal classes of countries: those whose conflicts are, for better or worse, of interest to rich countries capable of becoming involved in their resolution; and those countries about whose conflicts no one much cares. Such a division would not only openly tolerate the human costs of certain wars. It would also erode whatever deterrent power is slowly being built in the evolving system of collective security and international law.

It is important at this juncture for all governments to reiterate the principle of collective financial responsibility for UN peacekeeping, including the related costs of peace-enforcement, humanitarian, and other non-military activities. Because of the rising costs, however, it must be recognized that substantial voluntary contributions will be needed from countries which can afford them. Thus, within the framework of collective financing, there must be provision for the early identification of contributions for which countries would waive reimbursement. The nature of the contributions should be made clear in advance, so that the UN can budget around them. Alternatively, some or all of the financial responsibility for a peacekeeping operation could be explicitly delegated by the UN under Chapter VIII of the Charter to a regional organization, and thus not be borne by the UN. Either would have the effect of reducing the total assessed costs of UN peacekeeping.

However done, all the money spent for peacekeeping—whether assessed or donated—should be acknowledged, so that countries and regional organizations are adequately credited for their voluntary contributions. Over time, the record of voluntary contributions might be taken into account in revising the scale of mandatory assessments.

A flexible mix of such arrangements over the next few years is likely to be the only way the international system as a whole can raise the suddenly large sums anticipated for UN peacekeeping. Much thinking is needed about the precise mechanisms required to provide the resources needed. But the principle must be clear. For the basic system of collective security to work, the overriding objective should be collective financial responsibility, subject to certain ad hoc adjustments. These adjustments will depend upon the nature of the peacekeeping operation; the special concerns of regions and neighbors; and the capacity to pay.

2. Policy Recommendations for Trilateral Governments to Urge on the United Nations

a. Adjust assessment schedules and enhance financial reserves.
In order to make it easier for governments to meet their financial obligations, the UN should adjust its assessment schedules. For the regular budget the UN should divide the annual assessment due each January into quarterly installments due throughout the year. This would make it easier for countries to adjust their own fiscal years to that of the UN. Perhaps as the recent report of the Independent Advisory Group on UN Financing (hereinafter the "Ogata-Volcker" report) recommends, interest might then be charged on late payments.

Budgeting for peacekeeping requires even more drastic reorganization. In order to streamline the now almost incessant flow of assessments for separate peacekeeping operations, the UN should adopt a single annual budget for peacekeeping, as the Ogata-Volcker report and others have suggested. A single budget for peacekeeping would combine the special assessments levied for individual operations into one budget which would be financed, like the regular budget, with a single annual assessment. It too could be paid in quarterly installments. This would enable countries to predict the costs of peacekeeping and authorize the funds to meet them in advance. If, in a given year, the annual budget were greater than actual expenditures, governments would receive credit against the next year's assessment. If the budget underestimated the need, the UN could go to the members with an additional special assessment, just as it now does for every new mission.

The single peacekeeping budget would project the annual cost of all ongoing peacekeeping missions. It would also include common peacekeeping costs, such as stockpiles, training and the like. Finally, the single budget would include contingency funds for unanticipated missions.[37] Such contingency funds could not be expended without prior Security Council approval of a new operation and appropriation by the General Assembly, but they could be drawn upon for urgent start-up costs.

Once governments get current on their assessments and repay their arrears, the existing UN reserves will be replenished. At that juncture, governments should consider whether higher levels of reserves are needed for both the regular budget and for peacekeeping. The Ogata-Volcker report recommends an increase in the Working Capital Fund from $100 to $200 million and an increase in the Peacekeeping

Reserve Fund from its current level of $150 to $400 million.[38] These increases would be financed by mandatory assessments. This scale of increase and method of collection would seem to be appropriate targets for Trilateral governments to support. With reserves replenished and perhaps expanded, the UN should end the practice of borrowing from the balances in peacekeeping accounts in order to cover expenditures in the regular budget.[39]

b. Strengthen UN Headquarters capacity.
No matter how many resources governments are willing to earmark for UN use in future peacekeeping operations, the UN Secretariat itself needs to strengthen its capacities to plan and manage peacekeeping operations in a much more sophisticated manner. The rapid expansion of UN peacekeeping since 1988 has stretched the current system to the breaking point. There are those in UN Headquarters who are somewhat dubious about expanded capabilities, fearing both undue influence of certain governments in their design and the unwillingness of governments over time to provide adequate financial support.

It is no criticism of the valiant efforts of the UN Secretariat over the past few years to say that its capacities badly need strengthening. Many observers of the Secretariat, in and out of government, find its peacekeeping capabilities almost unbelievably small and obsolete: lacking the basic communications and management tools which even a small foreign or defense ministry in an industrialized country would take for granted.

The UN needs more resources of several types: (1) an operations center/situation room in the Secretariat, with real-time communications links to peacekeeping operations in the field; (2) strengthened planning, field operations and budgeting units within the Department of Peacekeeping Operations; (3) an expanded UN peacekeeping training program which is meshed with the training facilities now operated or planned by national governments and regional organizations; and (4) expanded UN stockpiles of equipment, including the capacities to stock and maintain communications gear and transport vehicles. New depots should be established in various regions of the world with pre-positioned equipment and stocks. These enhanced stockpiles would produce substantial returns in terms of timely start-ups for new peacekeeping missions.

In 1993 certain moves were taken in these directions including the creation of a situation room in the Department of Peacekeeping

Operations which can communicate with major UN operations 24 hours a day seven days a week, and a planning center in the Military Adviser's Office. The UN is also in the process of creating a network of peacekeeping training programs and facilities.

If the UN continues to strengthen its own military capacities in these various ways and governments provide regular funding for them, it will be easier for the Secretariat and government delegations to develop a common approach to future military needs. This, in turn, will give governments more confidence than they now have in the peacekeeping budgets which they are presented.

c. Revise the special peacekeeping scale of assessment.
As noted above, the fairness of the special assessment scale for peacekeeping is under vigorous discussion in the General Assembly. The immediate problem is that reduced assessments for Russia and the other republics of the former Soviet Union will require other industrial countries, and particularly the other Permanent Members of the Security Council, to pay increased assessments. During the 1992 U.S. political campaign, President Clinton called for the reduction of the U.S. assessment for peacekeeping from 30.4% to 25%, as have many members of the U.S. Congress. Now just the opposite is happening. The United States has already stated it will not pay more than its 1992 rate of 30.4% and is devising a strategy for lowering it.

One precondition of preserving the principle of collective financial responsibility for peacekeeping is that the burden-sharing must be seen to be equitable. Thus, at some time it will be necessary to recalculate the assessment scale so that countries pay no more, and no less, than their fair share.

There are various ways to recalculate the burdens. Both Secretary-General Boutros-Ghali and the Ogata-Volcker report endorse the principle that all UN members with above-average per capita incomes, except for the Permanent Members, should pay the same rate of assessment for peacekeeping and the regular budget.[40] Others suggest that much the same objective could be achieved by changing the number of groups into which states are classified or recalculating the percentages which they are asked to pay.

Whatever procedure is chosen, the criteria should be clear and kept current. The developing countries should continue to be assessed at a lower rate than the rest. The question of whether the "surcharge" on the five Permanent Members should be retained—potentially the most controversial question—can best be decided in connection with future decisions about changing the membership of the Security Council. If the surcharge is retained and permanent members increase in number, at least the burden would be more broadly shared and thus become less onerous.

d. Emphasize UN administration and management reform.
While UN reform is not the subject of this paper, it has been so closely linked to UN financing over the years that the subject must be raised.

It is clear that the willingness of governments to finance peacekeeping is greatly affected by their perceptions of the quality of UN administration and management. If governments or their citizens believe that quality control is lax and corruption or cheating rife, they will haggle over the smallest expenditures, perhaps with good cause. The level of corruption in the UN, including in its peacekeeping operations, may be grossly exaggerated in sensational newspaper articles. But it does exist. This has led to calls for an Inspector General and strengthened internal and external auditing systems which the UN would do well to accept.

The larger problems at the UN, however, are inefficiency, the lack of capacity, and the lack of transparency. These are not only the fault of the Secretariat. They must also be attributed to self-interested and often inappropriate demands which governments place on the Secretariat. To address these larger problems, major changes need to be made in the administrative, personnel and management practices at the UN. It would be advisable to establish an institution within the UN, comparable to the U.S. General Accounting Office, which could regularly analyze ongoing UN operations and propose improvements. The importance of appointing the most highly qualified persons to senior positions in the Department of Administration and Management at the UN cannot be overemphasized.

Trilateral countries can all contribute to improving the quality of the international civil service. They can encourage their best young graduates to pursue careers in the UN, as "the best and the brightest" did in the 1940s and 1950s. All governments should propose only their most distinguished citizens to high-level UN posts, and resist the temptation to solve domestic political problems by off-loading political leftovers onto the world organization. Trilateral governments should give special scholarship support to promising citizens of developing countries who wish to pursue UN careers.

In order to build long-term political and financial support for the United Nations, governments should continue to give the highest priority to promoting administrative and management reform and accountability at the UN. So, too, should the Secretary-General and his senior officials. However, for at least a certain period of time, governments should stop making financial support contingent on specific reforms. Governments should also remove the fiscal straitjacket of the zero growth budget, which has been in place since 1986 and has now become counterproductive. In sum, if governments become genuinely willing to cooperate with the Secretariat in strengthening the United Nations, reforms might become possible which are impossible under the current conditions of fixed resources, suspicious scrutiny and micro-management.

e. Consider long-term financial reforms.
The discussion above has dwelt upon incremental changes in current policies. We should not, however, be too cautious in our thinking. Governments face a substantially increased demand for UN peacekeeping over a prolonged period of time, as well as demands for other very large collective ventures, such as major undertakings for sustainable development. Thus, they should begin to think about new sources of UN financing, other than assessed or voluntary government contributions. Proposals to provide the UN with independent resources or direct flows of resources include: the establishment of substantial endowments; solicitation of contributions from private individuals and institutions; and international taxes on international air travel, shipping, global capital flows and the like.

At the moment, governments are unwilling to give the UN independent sources of funds. Not only would such funds reduce governments' ability to control the UN, they would also raise controversial ideological questions and invade national tax bases. The Ogata-Volcker report concludes that at this time, "current proposals for additional, nongovernmental sources of financing are neither practical nor desirable".[41]

However, if over time the effectiveness and efficiency of the UN increases, governments might be more willing to consider direct means of financing some activities of the UN. Thus, progress towards UN reform and accountability in the most general sense will contribute not only to the present, but also to the future, financial viability of the world organization. It is in everyone's interest that the UN, in making ends meet, can meet its ends.

APPENDIX
Current Methods of Financing the United Nations

The regular budget is financed according to the principle of collective financial responsibility, based on Article 17.2 of the Charter which holds that "[t]he expenses of the Organization shall be borne by the Members as apportioned by the General Assembly." Article 18 holds that the General Assembly exercises this budgetary power by a two-thirds majority vote. Full payment of UN assessments is a legally binding obligation on member states.[42]

The regular budget is financed according to a scale of assessments based on the principle of capacity to pay, with a maximum assessment of 25% established in 1971 and a minimum assessment of 0.01% established in 1978.[43] The assessment formula is based initially on a state's gross domestic product averaged over the preceding 10-year period and then adjusted downward for countries with high levels of external indebtedness or lower than average per capita income. States with low levels of indebtedness and higher than average per capita income pay a correspondingly higher rate of assessment. Since the United States would be assessed at approximately 27% on the basis of its gross domestic product, its rate is adjusted downwards to the 25% ceiling and other states pay correspondingly more.

The UN's regular biennial budget is prepared by the Secretariat and approved, after review by the Advisory Committee on Administrative and Budgetary Questions (ACABQ) and the Fifth Committee, by the General Assembly. Since 1986, as a result of intense pressure from major contributors led by the United States, General Assembly decisions to approve the budget have been made by consensus: thus granting each major contributor—but also every other nation—an effective veto over the budget.[44] Since 1986, the major contributors have also insisted on zero real growth in the UN's regular budget: limiting its growth basically to the rate of inflation and exchange rate fluctuations. This constraint is intended to wring out inefficiencies and duplication by forcing new UN initiatives to be financed by commensurate reductions in other, lower priority activities.

The regular budget includes the expenses of the major UN bodies: the General Assembly, the Security Council, the Economic and Social Council, the Secretariat and the International Court of Justice. Thus it supports the legal, administrative and other infrastructure required for mounting peacekeeping operations. It also provides the administrative costs of a number of UN development and humanitarian programs, such as the UN High Commissioner for Refugees (UNHCR).

Voluntary contributions support large operational programs of economic development and humanitarian assistance through agencies such as UNHCR, the United Nations Development Programme (UNDP) and the United Nations Children's Fund (UNICEF). The industrial countries are by far the largest contributors to these programs which, by tradition, were not deemed "core" and hence mandatory UN programs. Governments also make voluntary contributions to establish individual trust funds for specific purposes. These trust funds, directly administered by the UN, are often established when the UN initiates a program for which the General Assembly did not provide in the regular budget. Such specific purpose trust funds have increased over the past years and now number well over 100. Some, such as the Afghanistan Emergency Trust Fund, the Kampuchean Emergency Trust Fund and the new Central Emergency Fund provide humanitarian and economic assistance in specific conflict areas in which peacekeeping operations are deployed.

The UN has four sources of financial *reserves* for the regular budget and/or peacekeeping: the Working Capital Fund; the Special Account; the newly established Peacekeeping Reserve Fund, and certain temporarily-retained surpluses in both the regular budget and specific peacekeeping accounts.[45]

The Working Capital Fund was established in 1946 as a cash reserve. It enables the Secretary-General to meet day-to-day operating expenses until sufficient assessed payments for the regular budget are received and to meet "unforeseen and extraordinary" expenses, until such time as the General Assembly acts to meet them. Over time, the Working Capital Fund has been increased from $20 million in 1947 to $100 million in 1982.[46] In 1992 it equals approximately 9% of the regular budget and 4% of the combined regular and peacekeeping budgets. Since the mid-1980s, the Working Capital Fund has been regularly used to meet day-to-day obligations and to cover cash shortfalls due to late payment or non-payment of assessments.

The Special Account was established in 1965 as a mechanism into which member states could make voluntary contributions so as to rectify the financial crisis occasioned by withholdings of assessed contributions to the peacekeeping operations in the Suez and the Congo. It gave governments, which for reasons of principle had withheld their assessed contributions, a mechanism to support the UN without ceding on principle. As of 1992, the Special Account had grown to $140 million.[47] Since the mid-1980s, the Special Account has been used as if it were an additional Working Capital Fund.[48]

In 1992 the General Assembly established the Peacekeeping Reserve Fund at an authorized level of $150 million as a cash flow mechanism to meet temporary cash shortages in existing peacekeeping operations or the start-up costs of new peacekeeping operations. Of the $150 million total, $59 million has been transferred from unspent surpluses in the accounts of two peacekeeping operations: $42 million from the account of the United Nations Transition Assistance Group (UNTAG) in Namibia and $17 million from the account of the United Nations Iran-Iraq Military Observer Group (UNIIMOG) on the Iran-Iraq border. The Fund is already in use. The remaining $91 million is in principle provided from regular budget surpluses which the UN retained in 1987. In fact, these funds have been spent to cover member state arrears since 1987. They will actually become available in the Peacekeeping Reserve Fund only after member states pay their arrears and the Working Capital Fund and the Special Account are replenished.

Finally, there is the sum of various temporarily-held surpluses in the regular budget and in separate peacekeeping accounts. The United Nations is liable under its Financial Regulations to repay member states any balances in appropriations remaining after a financial period. The General Assembly can act to suspend these regulations and authorize the UN to temporarily retain the surpluses. It has done so with regard to the regular budget, UNEF II/UNDOF in Egypt and Syria and UNIFIL in Lebanon. As of September 30, 1992, these temporarily-held surpluses amounted to approximately $432 million.[49] However—with the exception of the funds targeted for the Peacekeeping Reserve Fund—the UN is obligated to return this amount to the member states as soon as sufficient assessments are collected to do so.

All told, the UN records approximately $670 million in these various reserves. In fact this is only "paper money," since outstanding assessments substantially exceed this amount. The Working Capital Fund, the Special Account and the Peacekeeping Reserve Fund can be replenished and temporarily-retained surpluses returned to member states only if states pay in full all arrears owed the United Nations for both the regular budget and various peacekeeping assessments.

NOTES

1. Boutros Boutros-Ghali, *Report on the Work of the Organization from the Forty-sixth to the Forty-seventh Session of the General Assembly*, DPI 1289 (United Nations, New York, September 1992), paragraph 15.
2. *Ibid.*, paragraph 19 for 1987 number. 1993 numbers from *Background Note, United Nations Peace-keeping Operations*, PS/DPI/15/Rev. 4 (United Nations, May 1993).
3. Security Council Document S/23500 (Declaration by the Heads of State and Government at the Summit Meeting of January 31, 1992), p. 3.
4. "Munich Economic Summit Political Declaration: Shaping the New Partnership," July 7, 1992, reproduced in *Weekly Compilation of Presidential Documents*, Monday July 13, 1992, Volume 28, Number 28, p. 1221.
5. Boutros Boutros-Ghali, *An Agenda for Peace: Preventive Diplomacy, Peacemaking and Peace-keeping, June 1992*, United Nations Department of Information (DPI) 1247, (United Nations, New York, 1992), paragraph 2.
6. Independent Advisory Group on U.N. Financing, "Financing an Effective United Nations: Report of the Independent Advisory Group on U.N. Financing" (The Ford Foundation, February 1993), p. 27.
7. John Stoessinger, *Financing the United Nations System* (The Brookings Institution, Washington, D.C., 1964), Chapters 5 and 6.
8. Susan R. Mills, "The Financing of United Nations Peacekeeping Operations: The Need for a Sound Financial Basis," *International Peace Academy Occasional Papers on Peacekeeping*, Number 3, 1989, p. 15ff.
9. *Ibid.* and *Information Notes on United Nations Peace-keeping Operations*, PS/DPI/18/Rev. 1 (United Nations, September 1992) and Security Council Resolution 831 of May 27, 1993.

10. ST/ADM/SER.B/403 of February 10, 1993 (Status of Contributions as at January 31, 1993).
11. See Vita Bite, "U.N. System Funding: Congressional Issues," *Congressional Research Service Issue Brief*, July 9, 1992, p. 6, and *Washington Weekly Report* of January 26, 1990, and February 2, 1990.
12. General Assembly Document A/C.5/47/13, *The Financial Situation of the United Nations: Report of the Secretary-General*, October 5, 1992, and ST/ADM/SER.B/411 of June 8, 1993 (Status of Contributions as at May 31, 1993).
13. ST/ADM/SER.B/411, *ibid.*
14. General Assembly Document A/C.5/47/13, *op. cit.*, p. 8, and Mills, *op. cit.*, p. 20ff.
15. General Assembly Document A/C.5/47/13, *ibid.*, and the statement of Richard Thornburgh to the Fifth Committee on October 13, 1992.
16. Mills, *op. cit.*, p. 21.
17. *Ibid.*, p. 8.
18. *Ibid.*, pp. 26-27.
19. See William J. Durch and Barry M. Blechman, *Keeping the Peace: The United Nations in the Emerging World Order* (The Henry L. Stimson Center, Washington, D.C., 1992), p. 62.
20. See General Assembly Document A/46/893 of March 13, 1992, *Financing of the United Nations Protection Force: Report of the Advisory Committee on Administrative and Budgetary Questions*, paragraph 32.
21. See General Assembly Resolution 46/187 of December 20, 1991.
22. See Durch and Blechman, *op. cit.*, *passim*, and Mills, *op. cit.*
23. See General Assembly Document A/47/733 of December 3, 1992, *Financing of the United Nations Transitional Authority in Cambodia: Report of the Secretary-General.*
24. See General Assembly Document A/47/607 of November 2, 1992, *Financing of the United Nations Operation in Somalia: Report of the Secretary-General.*
25. For the information on UNTAC, see General Assembly Resolution GA/RES/222A of February 14, 1992, and General Assembly Document A/46/235/Add.1 of January 31, 1992, *Financing of the United Nations Transitional Authority in Cambodia: Report of the Secretary-General.* For the information on UNPROFOR, see General Assembly Resolution GA/RES/233 of March 19, 1992; General Assembly Document A/46/893 of March 13, 1992, *Financing of the United Nations Protection Force: Report of the Advisory Committee on Administrative and Budgetary Questions*; and General Assembly Document A/46/236/Add.1 of March 6, 1992, *Financing of the United Nations Protection Force: Report of the Secretary-General.*
26. Mills, *op. cit.*
27. *Ibid.*, p. 26.
28. See, for example, United Nations Department of Public Information Press Release GA/AB/2797, October 19, 1992, on the 9th meeting of the Fifth Committee of the 47th General Assembly.
29. Gerald B. Helman and Steven R. Ratner, "Saving Failed States," *Foreign Policy*, Winter 1992-93, Number 89, pp. 3-20.
30. See Security Council Document S/25264/Corr. 1 of February 12, 1993.

31. See the statement by Barbara McDougall, Secretary of State for External Affairs, Canada, before the United Nations General Assembly, New York, September 24, 1992, and a statement by Ambassador Butler of Australia, U.N. Document GA/SPC/2046, November 12, 1992.

32. See Security Council Document S/25264 of February 10, 1993, *Further Report of the Secretary-General pursuant to Security Council Resolution 743 (1992)*, paragraphs 31 and 33.

33. See Security Council Resolution 815 of March 30, 1993, and Security Council documents S/25470 of March 25, 1993, and S/25470/Add.1 March 26, 1993, *Report of the Secretary General Pursuant to Security Council Resolution 807 (1993)*.

34. Independent Advisory Group, *op. cit.*, p. 10.

35. *An Agenda for Peace, op. cit.*, paragraph 48.

36. ST/ADM/SER.B/395, of January 5, 1993 (Status of Contributions as at December 31, 1992).

37. Independent Advisory Group, *op. cit.*, p. 19.

38. *Ibid.*, pp. 11 and 18.

39. *Ibid.*, p. 18.

40. *Ibid.*, p. 20 and General Assembly Document A/47/484, *op. cit.*, paragraphs 8 and 9.

41. Independent Advisory Group, *ibid.*, p. 23.

42. Stoessinger, *op. cit.*, and Jose E. Alvarez, "Legal Remedies and the United Nations à la carte problem," *Michigan Journal of International Law*, Volume 12, Number 2, Winter 1991, pp. 229-311.

43. See General Assembly Document A/46/11 Addendum 2, Supplement Number 11, September 23, 1991 (Report of the Committee on Contributions).

44. See General Assembly Resolution 41/213 of December 19, 1986.

45. General Assembly Document A/46/600/Add.1 of 19 November 1991, *The Financial Situation of the United Nations, Proposals to address the problems of today and tomorrow: Report of the Secretary-General*, p. 24.

46. Mills, *op. cit.*, pp. 13-15.

47. General Assembly Document A/C.5/47/13, *op. cit.*

48. *Ibid.*, pp. 12-13.

49. *Ibid.* and General Assembly Document A/46/600/Add.1, *op. cit.*

IV. Trilateral Country Roles: Challenges and Opportunities

Masashi Nishihara

Trilateral countries today are engaged in multilateral peacekeeping activities more actively than ever before. We form a critical core of the peace efforts being undertaken or supported by the United Nations. Trilateral countries provided about one-half of deployed UN peacekeeping forces at the end of 1992, or about two-thirds if the U.S.-led forces in Somalia are included (see Table 4). Our countries take the lead in the debates in the Security Council and other international fora and formulate frameworks for UN and UN-supported operations. As regional conflicts grow in size and number and complexity, making multilateral peacekeeping efforts more effective has become a key task for us.

Because of the kind of resources they have available and because of historical and political constraints imposed on them, different Trilateral countries have played different international peacekeeping roles. Are these roles likely to change in the near future? What key challenges do particular Trilateral countries face in strengthening multilateral peacekeeping efforts? In what way can we work together to make these multilateral efforts stronger?

Trilateral countries may be classified into three categories in terms of the kind of roles they play in multilateral peacekeeping activities: "full-fledged traditional peacekeepers," "self-restrained peacekeepers," and "peace-enforcers." These may be described briefly as follows:

- "Full-fledged traditional peacekeepers" have historically set the model for UN peacekeeping operations (PKO). Those Trilateral countries which are small to middle-sized, and which during the Cold War period either maintained neutralist foreign policies or sought more or less autonomous policies within the Western alliance, tend to come under this category. Canada, the Nordic countries, Belgium, the Netherlands, Austria, Ireland and Italy have played this role.

TABLE 4
Trilateral Contributions to UN Peacekeeping Operations
(as of December 31, 1992)

	Civilian Police	Troops	Military Observers	Total
Europe	727	19,120	788	20,610
Austria	22	798	42	862
Belgium	—	821	18	839
Denmark	40	1,210	50	1,300
Finland	—	1,197	43	1,240
France	172	6,206	124	6,502
Germany	76	145	—	221
Greece	—	—	7	7
Ireland	20	686	54	760
Italy	85	49	25	159
Luxembourg	—	37	—	37
Netherlands	14	1,859	61	1,934
Norway	53	1,053	60	1,166
Portugal	35	—	12	47
Spain	119	768	124	1,011
Sweden	91	604	57	752
Switzerland	—	43	11	54
United Kingdom	—	3,644	75	3,719
Canada	45	3,172	68	3,285
United States	—	344	92	436
Japan	75	600	8	683
TRILATERAL TOTAL (A)	847	23,236	956	25,014
WORLD TOTAL (B) (67 countries)	4,413	45,675	2,066	52,154
TRILATERAL SHARE OF WORLD TOTAL (A/B)	19%	51%	46%	48%

Source: United Nations, "Summary of Contributions to Peace-keeping Operations by Countries as of 31 December 1992"

Note: This table does not include multilateral operations which, while approved by the Security Council, are not under UN command. The largest such operation at the end of 1992 was in Somalia, where there were some 550 Belgian military personnel, some 1,500 to 2,000 French military personnel, and some 28,000 U.S. troops. If Somalia were included in the above table, the share of personnel provided by Trilateral countries would rise to about two-thirds.

- "Self-restrained peacekeepers" have just begun to participate in UN peacekeeping operations with self-restraint. Germany and Japan are in this category. Both are trying to overcome the historical legacy of militarism and popular pacifist sentiments, although Germany has expanded its military role since the Constitutional Court's favorable decision to that effect in early April 1993.

- "Peace-enforcers" are willing to deploy more assertive coercive measures under UN mandate, or to strengthen UN functions by substantiating Chapter VII of the UN Charter. The United States, the United Kingdom, and France are the key countries in this category.

This categorization is admittedly oversimplified. Canada, for instance, has troops in the former Yugoslavia and in Somalia playing roles beyond those of traditional peacekeepers, since they are deployed where cease-fires are virtually non-existent. Germany has taken up peace-enforcing missions in ex-Yugoslavia. The United States has sent military observers under UNPKO, the first category. The United Kingdom and France have had forces in Cyprus and south Lebanon for a number of years. Nonetheless, these three categories are useful in discussing the challenges we are facing today.

A. FULL-FLEDGED TRADITIONAL PEACEKEEPERS: CHANGING MISSIONS, DIFFICULT ISSUES

During the Cold War era when regional conflicts were often aggravated by the larger East–West rivalry, traditional peacekeepers contributed significantly to international peace by monitoring cease-fire arrangements and separating combatants. They are proud of their record, and justifiably so. Many of the peacekeepers began to be engaged in a prototype of peacekeeping back in 1948, long before Lester B. Pearson, then Canada's Minister for External Affairs and a future Prime Minister, advanced the concept of "interpositional peacekeeping." Based on that Canadian concept advanced during the Suez Crisis of 1956, Dag Hammarskjöld, a Swedish diplomat, as UN Secretary-General, in 1958 formulated guiding principles for such peacekeeping activities by the UN that set a basic framework for subsequent UN efforts.

With the end of the Cold War and the emergence of a new, more uncertain era, traditional peacekeepers are even more willing to take part in resolving regional conflicts and maintaining regional peace. However, sending their troops into potentially risky areas always raises new and difficult issues of interests, resources, and options.

1. Canada

Canada's debates and policies present typical problems traditional peacekeepers are facing today. The Canadians have positively participated in all UN peacekeeping operations since 1956 and in many embryonic UN missions prior to that. Canada is one of the first countries that established within its armed forces a standby force available for UN peacekeeping missions on short notice.

Yet, given the increasing number of regional conflicts that require UN involvement today, Canadians ask what criteria they should apply in deciding which missions they should take up. During the Cold War there was a fairly clear criterion: to help reduce East–West tensions enhances Canada's national security. In contrast, not all of today's regional conflicts so directly affect Canadian security. Canadians will find it very hard to set criteria for selective participation. They also debate how they should adjust essential aspects of their peacekeeping efforts—namely, personnel, finance, material, education and training—so as best to meet the changing needs.

As of December 31, 1992, about 3,300 Canadian troops, about 6.3% of total UN forces, were engaged in 12 different UN operations. Canada has been responsive to the UN request for missions in Somalia, Macedonia, and Mozambique. Early this year it sent some 900 troops to Somalia, thus making a total of about 4,300 participants. If Ottawa desires to maintain the current level of commitment, it requires a big increase in its 1993-94 defense budget. UN efforts already take up an estimated 20 to 25 percent of the current defense budget. This is large, particularly when set against the deep cuts in the 1992 defense budget. Peacekeeping efforts for 1992 were C$170 million (US$135 million) over budget, since Canada contributed some 2,400 troops to the former Yugoslavia and paid the full cost for them.

Despite strains on financial resources, Canada is likely to keep up its support of UN peace efforts by adjusting its deployment policies. Canadians may increase their level of participation at the expense of other military commitments. Canada has begun to reduce its 580 troops stationed in Cyprus and withdrawn its troops from NATO missions in Germany, which it has redeployed in ex-Yugoslavia. Another option may be—as proposed by General John de Chastelain, then chief of defense staff and now Ambassador to the United States—to dispatch a large number of troops at the outset of UN operations as a kind of rapid deployment force and then to reduce them as other national contingents arrive.

Whichever option Canada may take, it is departing from the role of a traditional peacekeeper who adheres to impartiality, non-coercion, and consent of host parties as principles of participation in UN peace efforts. Under a UN mandate it is willing to go into areas where cease-fires are not established. As it did in the Gulf War, Canada, accepting the authorization of the Security Council to act under Article 42 of the Charter, participates in Somalia with armored fighting vehicles.

2. European Peacekeepers

To a large extent, Canada's challenges are shared by most traditional full-fledged European peacekeepers, notably, Denmark, Sweden, Norway, Finland, the Netherlands, Belgium, Austria and Ireland. Spain is a newcomer, but has deployed sizable forces in Central America and ex-Yugoslavia. Like Canada, these countries have had strong commitments to UN peace efforts. The Nordic countries' commitments have been particularly commendable. They established standby forces for the UN to use, and have historically provided about one-third of total UN troops at any given time. Norway's Prime Minister Brundtland stressed in her UN speech in September 1992 that her country had cumulatively contributed 35,000 personnel in a total of 16 UN operations. A total of 28,000 Finnish troops have served on UN missions since 1956.

At the end of 1992, the European countries mentioned above had a total of about 9,300 peacekeepers participating in 12 UN operations. (85 percent of Norway's legally authorized maximum of 1,330 troops are now serving on active duty for UN peace efforts.) Despite limitations of human and financial resources, they have faithfully fulfilled their financial obligations to the UN. However, many feel today that their financial capacities are overstretched. They are high-cost countries and have to bear the full expenses for their operations, since the UN cannot for the time being reimburse the normal share of the expenses incurred for UN operations. Yet these countries are considering increasing the size of standby forces. Norway, for example, is increasing its legally authorized maximum from 1,330 to 2,000.

Other countries like the Netherlands are reducing, and plan to reduce further, their defense budgets and the size of their armed forces, and face the problem of how to readjust the missions of their forces to handle crisis management, such as the humanitarian and peacekeeping operations in Somalia. The Dutch plan to abolish conscription by 1998, and their forces will decrease from 125,000 at present to 70,000 at the turn of the century. They have announced they will refocus their defense efforts on peacekeeping missions.

Again, like Canada, many of the traditional, full-fledged European peacekeepers recognize the urgent need to assume functions of peace-enforcers. Denmark, for instance, dispatched a corvette as part of U.S.-led multinational coalition forces conducting a naval blockade against Iraq during the Gulf War. (This function was a limited application of Article 42 of the Charter, in that it involved non-combat aspects of peace-enforcement actions.) Sweden is debating whether its forces should accept peace-enforcing functions as well. Belgium has decided to play a peace-enforcer role by dispatching 550 paracommandos to Somalia.

As traditional full-fledged peacekeepers move to assume more risky missions, they will have to readjust the training of their troops, and reconsider their equipment.

B. SELF-RESTRAINED PEACEKEEPERS: BETWEEN DOMESTIC CONSTRAINTS AND INTERNATIONAL PRESSURE

Germany and Japan are two powers whose capabilities have been underused for multilateral peacekeeping efforts. Their constitutional constraints and anti-militarist sentiments, which stem from their pre-1945 legacies of militarism, are well-known, but without constitutional change, both have gradually broadened their international roles. The constitutional constraints depend very much on how the relevant provisions are interpreted, as many of the constraints are implicit rather than explicit. Both countries are now trying to overcome their constraints, for they desire to demonstrate their willingness to share the international burden of peacekeeping. Since the Constitutional Court's historic clarification in early April 1993, Germany has taken significant steps ahead of Japan. The two countries, in this sense, now face different rather than similar issues.

1. Germany

The constitutional challenge that faced the pre-unification Federal Republic with regard to participation in international peacekeeping activities continues in the post-unification period. The domestic debates this year were quite intense until April 8, threatening even a possible breakup of the precarious coalition government which Chancellor Helmut Kohl's Christian Democratic Union (CDU) and the Bavarian Christian Social Union (CSU) have formed with Count Otto Lambsdorff's Free Democratic Party (FDP).

The crux of the issue was not whether Germany could dispatch military personnel overseas to play the role of traditional full-fledged peacekeepers in UN operations. There is broad consensus among the ruling parties and the opposition Social Democratic Party (SPD) on this point. Although historically the West Germans were reluctant to become directly involved in UN peacekeeping activities, they gradually did so, beginning with financial contributions in the 1960s, and, in the 1970s, placing equipment and transport facilities at the UN's disposal. This was followed by sending civilian personnel to Nicaragua and Namibia in 1989, and non-combat military personnel (doctors) to Cambodia last year.

The question was whether Germany could dispatch its "combat" troops outside the NATO area without revising the Basic Law, to participate in both UN peacekeeping operations and UN-sanctioned military actions. This problem required an imminent resolution, since the Kohl government was being criticized by the SPD over its plan to take up a mission under Chapter VII of the UN Charter. The Chancellor intended to allow German peacekeeping and peace-enforcing roles "outside the NATO area" under UN resolutions, by allowing German participation in NATO early-warning surveillance planes (AWACS) in Hungarian and ex-Yugoslav skies that would help implement a Security Council decision to enforce the "no-fly zone" in Bosnia-Herzegovina, and by sending 1,500 troops, including infantry, for UN peacekeeping operations in Somalia after cease-fires are established.

Both the FDP and the SPD argued that such "out of the NATO area" military operations were unconstitutional, although the two had different reasons. The FDP took the position that Germany should participate in UN-supported combat operations, but only under a revised Basic Law or clarification by the Constitutional Court, whichever could give explicit authorization. The SPD insisted and still insists, however, that the constitution should be revised to forbid Germany's involvement in any combat missions outside the NATO area. Chancellor Kohl and FDP Chairman Lambsdorff in mid-January of this year introduced a bill to amend the Basic Law to allow German forces to participate in (1) traditional UN peacekeeping operations, (2) UN-sanctioned peace-enforcement operations, and (3) joint actions under international institutions such as NATO, WEU, and CSCE. However, faced with the possible imminent need to enforce the UN-sanctioned "no-fly zone" in Bosnia with the involvement of NATO AWACS aircraft, the Chancellor shifted his stand to favor German pilots flying on these AWACS planes under the present constitution. This led the FDP to threaten to withdraw from the coalition government unless the Constitutional Court authorized it. The Constitutional Court, on April 8, made a historic interim decision to support Kohl's position, by stating that continuing Germany's self-imposed restrictions on its military role would "endanger the trust for Germany" within the NATO alliance.

Although the Court's decision was an interim one applying only to the individual case and did not provide an authoritative interpretation of the disputed clauses in Germany's Basic Law, Chancellor Kohl has strengthened Germany's international credibility. Subsequently, on April 20, he also announced a decision to send about 1,600 German troops to Somalia in June.

The Kohl government's concern is, first, Germany's international status. To be a permanent member of the UN Security Council, he realizes, his country has to be able to act under Chapter VII of the UN Charter. Second, if it wants to staunch the inflow of political refugees and economic migrants fleeing the chaos in its eastern and southern neighbors, Germany needs to be able to prevent wider conflicts by using its forces as part of regional and international efforts rather than by taking independent action. Germany could not effectively urge such efforts on other countries unless it was itself willing to make appropriate military contributions.

This does not mean, however, that Germany would send ground troops for combat missions, if supported by the UN, into the former Yugoslavia in the near future. There is still strong fear among the Germans that their country might get involved in the messy ethnic and regionalist conflicts there. Nonetheless, Germany has ceased being "a self-restrained peacekeeper" and is on its way to entering the group of "peace-enforcers."

This shift reflects the drastic change on the part of international opinion toward Germany that has occurred over the last few years. During the Gulf War not many countries in Europe really wanted to see Germany participating in coalition forces with combat missions. However, now with the ongoing traumas unfolding in the former Yugoslavia and Somalia, and with Germany's economic and military capabilities being substantial, many regard German power as underutilized.

2. Japan

Similarly underutilized is Japanese power. Japan joined the UN in 1956 and has since emphasized supporting and strengthening the UN in its foreign policy. Yet the government did not join UN peacekeeping operations for 36 years, until June 1992, when the parliament finally passed the UNPKO Cooperation Law. The pacifist sentiment at home and Asian fears of a possible revival of Japanese militarism are still critical restraining factors on Japan's participation in UN peace efforts. As the German government did, the Japanese government began with financial contributions and then sent civilian personnel after 1989, before finally introducing the PKO bill in the Diet.

The PKO Cooperation Law does not allow Japanese forces to perform what other Trilateral countries regard as normal, full-fledged peacekeeping functions. The law refers to "normal" or full-fledged peacekeeping functions such as supervising cease-fires, patrolling demilitarized zones, disarming hostile forces, and removing mines. However, to secure majority support for the bill in the upper house of the Diet, the government acceded to the demands of the two centrist opposition parties, the Democratic Socialist Party and the Clean Government (Komei) Party, to "freeze" the application of "dangerous" provisions until the Diet defreezes them. As a result Japan did not send infantry contingents to Cambodia but only an engineering battalion and a few military observers.

The law includes several other serious constraints, one of which is the restriction that Japanese forces can be sent only where cease-fires have been already established. Under this provision, Japanese troops cannot go to Somalia or the former Yugoslavia where there is no clear cease-fire among the warring parties. Yet, at the time of writing, at the strong request of the UN and the United States, Tokyo is trying to find ways to participate in "safe" transport functions in Somalia. The government will have to contend with the opposition parties to justify its involvement in Somalia. The government has decided to send about 50 troops to Mozambique for "transport control missions," now that there will be a cease-fire agreement there.

Despite these constraints, Japan's financial role should be mentioned as a positive note. The multinational coalition forces could not operate against Saddam Hussein in 1990–91 without substantial financial contributions from Japan, as well as from Germany, Saudi Arabia, and Kuwait. Similarly for the first phase of operations in Somalia, Japan pledged $100 million, a quarter of the UN trust fund to cover transportation, equipment and subsistence costs of participating forces unable to pay their own way.

Asian countries have often expressed their suspicion that Japan's participation in UN peacekeeping operations could be a springboard for a return to military power. Since a Japanese contingent started its mission in Cambodia in September 1992, this suspicion seems to have faded away, at least on the surface. South Korea and China have stopped criticizing Japan on this score. In fact, when Prime Minister Miyazawa visited ASEAN capitals in January 1993, the ASEAN leaders endorsed the Japanese role in the peace process in Cambodia. Manila has even asked Japan to help transport the equipment for its forces in Cambodia from the Philippines.

Like many Germans, many Japanese aspire to see their country attain a permanent seat in the UN Security Council. However, the fact that Japan is not ready to take up normal peacekeeping obligations, much less responsibilities under Chapter VII of the Charter, narrows its chances of attaining that status in the world body. Tokyo must build up a public consensus in support of its willingness to play an active role for international security, which has been impeded by constitutional debates centered around the no-war clause (Article 9) of the constitution.

Constitutional debates in Japan, which have been even more "theological" than those in Germany, have emphasized constraints more than opportunities. There are four major issues: (1) How extensively can Japan extend the scope of its right to individual self-defense? (2) Can Japan constitutionally exercise the right of collective self-defense (defending its ally under Article 51 of the UN Charter)? (3) Can Japan use force as part of UN peacekeeping operations (Chapter "VI and a half" of the Charter)? (4) Can Japan play its part in enforcing collective security (deploying its troops under a UN command under Chapter VII of the Charter)?

Since the Gulf War, during which Japan had agonizing experiences of not being able to contribute military personnel, constitutional debate has intensified. Since last fall several influential Liberal Democratic Party members and a growing number of moderate intellectuals have started to argue that the 1946 Constitution should be amended to explicitly allow the Self-Defense Forces to play an international peacekeeping role. In the meantime, a former LDP party secretary, Ichiro Ozawa, advocates that Japan under the present constitution can and should contribute its forces under a UN command. The ruling party's Constitutional Research Council began in February this year to deliberate on possible constitutional revision, despite the strong opposition of Prime Minister Miyazawa.

How far this constitutional debate will go remains to be seen. Since there is no constitutional court in Japan like in Germany, it may be more realistic to give a more flexible interpretation to the constitution, rather than to try to revise it, to find ways to elevate Japan to a full-fledged peacekeeper and to participation in non-combat functions of UN-sanctioned peace-enforcing missions.

C. PEACE-ENFORCERS:
FROM U.N.-SANCTIONED TO U.N.-COMMANDED?

1. The United States

The United States is in a way a newcomer to UN operations. During the Cold War era, it was virtually unable to take a neutral role in the way traditional peacekeepers did, although it did send a few military observers under UN peacekeeping operations. Unlike Germany and Japan, the United States has no constitutional constraint on the kind of role it may play in the field of international security, although the respective roles of the Executive and the Congress in sending U.S. forces into combat are not fully defined despite the "war powers resolution" of the 1970s. Washington chose to begin with peace-enforcing operations. In 1990, faced with the Iraqi invasion and annexation of Kuwait, it led the UN Security Council to support the deployment of multinational coalition forces against Saddam Hussein. This was the first peace-enforcing operation of its kind, undertaken with the support of the UN Security Council, in the post-Cold War period.

In December 1992 the United States again took the initiative in deploying a sizable force of about 28,000 troops to Somalia with the endorsement of the UN Security Council, to get food supplies through to starving people caught in the endless civil war. This is a clear departure from the previous assumption that humanitarian intervention should be conducted in a non-coercive manner. The massive intervention in Somalia by the United States, with offers of assistance from about 35 other nations with varying missions, sets a precedent for future crises of this kind—although the case is highly unusual in that no effective Somali government existed.

With these precedents, the Americans are searching for ways to strengthen the collective security role of the UN. President Bush in his speech before the UN General Assembly in September 1992 stressed the importance of "strengthening the UN ability to prevent, contain and resolve conflict across the globe." The U.S. Senate Committee on Foreign Relations in September 1992 adopted a "Collective Security Participation Resolution" which recommended that the United States make a certain number of forces available to the United Nations under Article 43 of the Charter. Several American thinktank reports have also made recommendations along these lines. The UN Participation Act of 1945 can serve as the legal basis for deploying such standby forces. If this were done, it would be a new chapter for the UN.

However, before making arrangements for standby forces to be available to the UN, it seems that the Americans have to sort out for themselves to what extent they are willing to place their forces under a non-American UN commander. There have already been American military observers under foreign command, as in the case of the MFO in the Sinai, where a Norwegian general is now in charge. However, if the operation is large-scale and dangerous and depends principally on U.S. forces, as in the cases of the Gulf War and Somalia, the U.S. government has felt that only the United States can provide an effective command and control structure. If U.S. forces go to Bosnia as part of a UN-sanctioned, NATO-commanded force, or remain in Somalia in considerable numbers under UN command, these questions of command and balance among national contingents will have entered a new phase.

Smaller-scale peacekeeping forces under the UN are already less of a problem for the United States. At the time of writing, Washington is planning to send to Mozambique an engineering battalion which will have blue helmets. This is a new development. In fact, President Bush in September 1992 offered to make available American bases and facilities for multinational training and field exercises, expressing the U.S. government's strong interest in strengthening UN peacekeeping operations.

The Clinton Administration will have the important task of linking America's lift, communications, logistics, and intelligence capabilities to an enhanced UN role. The United States has to continue at times to play the role of chief policeman or peace-enforcer, for someone has to be in charge of each military intervention. Acceptance of that role serves as a catalyst for involving the world community on a broader scale. But under what circumstances and how often will the United States be willing to play this role of catalyst?

2. European Peace-Enforcers

The European peace-enforcers, the United Kingdom and France, have also been involved in traditional UN peacekeeping missions for many years. The United Kingdom was an original participant in UN operations in Cyprus in 1964, as France was with the UN Truce Supervision Organization in Lebanon in 1948. As of December 1992 the United Kingdom was contributing about 3,700 troops for five UN peacekeeping missions, and France about 6,500 in seven such missions. In the UN Protection Force in the former Yugoslavia alone, they have nearly 3,300 and 4,500 troops, respectively.

Nonetheless, Britain and France have also been the major European peace-enforcers. In the UN-authorized Operation Desert Storm, Britain and France deployed 42,000 and 12,000 troops, respectively. In January 1993 British and French forces joined the U.S. forces in attacking missile sites and military factories in Iraq, again under UN authorization. While the British and the French are enjoying their reputation as responsible permanent members of the UN Security Council with dangerous peace-enforcing roles under Chapter VII of the Charter, they feel that it is costing them much financially and stretching their capabilities virtually to the limit.

In 1992 Britain tripled its troop contribution to UN peacekeeping operations. But in a speech in January 1993 British Foreign Secretary Douglas Hurd said, "We shall probably have to say 'no' more often than 'yes'." Because of strains in financial and human resources, London decided not to send troops to Somalia although it contributed four transport aircraft and humanitarian aid. However, in February 1993 Britain announced that it would revise its original troop reduction plan, intended to bring the force level down to 116,000 by the mid-1990s, by adding 5,000 personnel to meet the growing needs of UN peacekeeping operations.

In 1992 Paris spent FFr2.5 billion (about $500 million) just for ex-Yugoslavia and Cambodia, which some suggest led it in September last year to cancel FFr2 billion (about $400 million) of spending previously appropriated for procurement of equipment. Peacekeeping roles also involve human sacrifice. In ex-Yugoslavia France has already lost more than 10 soldiers. As in the United States, the need to clarify the nature of missions and rules of engagement, and establish national interest priorities, is felt acutely. The French call for their government to have a clear political will to contain civil war and human calamity. To be motivated by humanitarian concerns without clear vision of a political outcome, however, would be nothing but an invitation to diplomatic disaster, many argue, and also risks the prestige and credibility of the UN. France deployed 2,100 troops in the midst of a rift between the Socialist Government's Defense and Humanitarian Ministers on this issue.

France has gone a step further than the United States in strengthening the UN capability. Recently it offered to make 1,000 troops available on 24-hours' notice to the UN and 2,000 troops within a week. This is a hopeful step toward implementing Article 43 of the Charter. As was mentioned before, Germany now has its Constitutional Court's support for participation in UN-sanctioned air reconnaissance missions. It has joined the "peace-enforcers."

A few other active traditional peacekeepers—Italy, Belgium, and Canada—need mentioning as peace-enforcers. Italy sent two battleships and ten fighter aircraft to the Gulf War. For Somalia, Rome has sent about 1,500 troops, which include marines, paratroopers, and support units. Belgium dispatched some 550 paratroopers, as was mentioned before, although it set the condition that its troops would stay for only a year. Ottawa subsequently sent about 900 troops, equipped with armored personnel carriers and armored fighting vehicles. Humanitarian concerns have driven these traditional peacekeepers to playing more risky roles.

D. PROMOTING TRILATERAL COOPERATION

As discussed above, Trilateral countries have played and are playing different roles in UN peace efforts. Today we are going through intense internal debates about how our international roles should be changed to meet the needs of the time. We are being challenged by our own limited financial and human resources, by historical and constitutional constraints, and by the burst of new regional conflicts seriously requiring humanitarian attention. Within these general constraints, we are nonetheless observing a dynamic process in which we are broadening our respective roles. How can we make multilateral efforts more effective? Since the question of how to finance peace efforts is discussed in Enid Schoettle's chapter, the following proposals treat other aspects of Trilateral cooperation.

1. Agree on a target number of forces available for
UN operations, and submit forces and their capabilities.

Trilateral countries should agree on a target number of armed forces which each can contribute for UN operations. This agreement can be first reached among the G-7 countries in consultation with the UN

Secretary-General—or it can be done among NATO members.

As regional conflicts which require UN and UN-supported intervention grow in number and scope, it would facilitate the work of the UN Security Council and the Secretary General if they know in advance the forces and the capabilities that they can count on from UN member states—particularly from Trilateral countries, which tend to have better equipment and are able to move faster. The Trilateral countries of necessity will have to provide core support for UN peacekeeping forces.

Our countries should submit to the UN what we can offer in terms of combat forces, communications, intelligence, and humanitarian aid—and how swiftly we can make these capabilities available. As mentioned earlier, the French have offered 1,000 troops to be dispatched on one day's notice for the UN. This strengthens UN preventive diplomacy, since these forces can be deployed to areas of tensions before they become more volatile.

2. With the target mentioned above in mind, explore and develop human and material resources fully for peacekeeping, peace-enforcing, and humanitarian operations.

Each of us should make further efforts in developing our potential capabilities to meet the rising needs of regional conflict resolution and to support multilateral efforts. For some, the main focus may be to reorganize and retrain forces for such purposes, and to provide new equipment. For others, it may be to introduce a "peacekeeping curriculum" at military schools. For still others, it may be to revise the constitution or to adopt new legislation, in order to facilitate their forces playing a more active role. For many, it may be to build up stockpiles of resources needed to cope with extensive famines and human rights violations caused by civil wars and border tensions. And perhaps for all our countries, it will be to adapt intellectually to the need for creative thinking about how to prevent regional crises and massive humanitarian disasters.

3. Promote efficient use of each other's capabilities.

Trilateral countries should study how to promote sharing some members' special capabilities for multilateral operations and how to minimize redundancy in our capabilities. For example, countries such as the United States, Great Britain, and France have superior lift capabilities, which can be used efficiently to transport troops of other national contingents. There have been precedents for Trilateral countries working for non-Trilateral countries. For example, the U.S. air force lifted 500 Pakistani UN peacekeepers to Mogadishu in September 1992. Japanese transports have helped transport some of the equipment and relevant materials of Philippine contingents for their activities in Cambodia.

Participating forces for multilateral operations tend to bring in overlapping capabilities such as medical services. While language and other issues may make mutual use of such facilities difficult, sharing of such services is cost-saving. It is being done in many cases, but it can be done more extensively through better coordination, at a time when financial constraints often impede the decision to dispatch troops.

We should prepare lists of our lift capabilities and other services available for such operations. We can even have agreements in advance, rather than negotiating only after the need arises. This may encourage joint planning and interoperability of equipment, which are also desirable for multinational cooperation.

4. Share training and exercise facilities.

UN peacekeeping requires training, and its multinational nature demands joint training. Traditionally Nordic countries have provided training courses for prospective peacekeepers of the European nations. Recently Norway and Sweden provided a seminar for personnel from East and Central Europe. In preparing to go to Cambodia, about 35 Japanese officers went to training programs in Sweden. The program included intensive instruction on the international law associated with UN peacekeeping operations and exercises on supervising cease-fires and disarming hostile forces.

The UN-associated International Peace Academy has provided many useful training programs for peacekeepers. In his UN speech in September 1992, President Bush offered American bases and facilities for multinational training and field exercises. More recently the Japanese government has also shown interest in the idea of establishing a joint PKO training center in Japan. Canada has briefed many foreign officers either in its country or abroad on UN peacekeeping missions. It is also interested in the possible establishment of an international PKO training center.

With the multiplicity of UN involvements in peacekeeping, several kinds of training centers with specialized programs would be useful. Nordic countries may stress training for "traditional peacekeeping" operations, and Canada and the United States may specialize in training of "restrained combat units" as well as engineering and logistical units. NATO and WEU could establish such a center, too. A training center in Japan or elsewhere in Asia may specialize in training for Asian languages, cultures, and climates.

These training centers need to standardize training manuals and equipment, which will be highly useful for enhanced Trilateral cooperation.

5. Add new UN-sanctioned missions to regional security institutions.

NATO and WEU are engaged in UN peacekeeping operations in ex-Yugoslavia, and peace-enforcing missions as well in containing the Serbs in Bosnia (enforcing the "no-fly zone"). The EC and CSCE are engaged in mediation and preventive diplomacy related to the Balkans. Though NACC features more as a political dialogue forum, its members have since December 1992 agreed to cooperate on peacekeeping operations. This will involve Russia and help build confidence between Western Europe and Central-Eastern Europe.

Similar missions may be added to Japanese-U.S. security arrangements. The Japanese and Americans may explore the possibility of jointly using those resources that are under the Security Treaty for peacekeeping efforts under a UN mandate. Non-military materials (such as prefabricated housing materials, printing machines, office equipment, and medical equipment), which may be needed for the swift introduction of UN civilian and military personnel into a new mission area, may be stockpiled or "prepositioned" in a Japanese or U.S. base in Japan and then transported quickly to necessary sites in Asia. An advance agreement between Japan and the United States in which Japanese troops can use American bases in Diego Garcia and other military facilities would also greatly help Japan overcome its own severely limited lift capabilities in participating in distant UN peacekeeping operations. Japan can in turn agree to provide other services such as fuel supply.

6. Develop dialogue with Russia and China on UN peacekeeping operations.

Finally, one of the important roles that Trilateral countries can play is more actively to develop dialogue with Russia and China, two permanent members of the UN Security Council whose resources have remained seriously underutilized for multilateral peacekeeping efforts. We need to engage them, both formally and informally, in an international sharing of the political and military burden in a way that ensures their support of UN peace efforts. Russia contributed only a little over 1,000 personnel as of the end of 1992. Likewise, China fielded less than 500 under a UN flag. China abstained in the UN Security Council on the resolution on the Gulf War. Moscow's interest in the possibility of placing its forces under NATO command in Bosnia is an encouraging development. While our roles constitute a core of UN peace efforts, we should try to obtain fuller cooperation from the two large powers which may become critical to peacekeeping efforts in parts of Eurasia.

V. Maintaining Broad Legitimacy for United Nations Action

Olara A. Otunnu

There is a sense in which the United Nations (UN) is but a microcosm of the "real world" of governments and their policies; as such it reflects more or less directly the realities in that world. Thus, while the Cold War lasted, the effectiveness of the world body was compromised, especially with regard to its principal mandate for maintaining international peace and security. The end of the Cold War has signaled at least three developments with far-reaching impact on the role of the Security Council, the UN body entrusted with primary responsibility for keeping the peace.

First and foremost, the Security Council has been set free. Freed from the East-West gridlock that paralyzed action, the Security Council is for the first time in a position to fulfill the role envisaged for it under the Charter. With its new-found activism, the scope of its decisions, and the increasingly intrusive character of the measures being adopted, the "new" Security Council resembles a miniature world government.

The second development is the rearrangement of power relations in the world, which is reflected directly in the Security Council. Soviet superpower has been replaced by a relatively weak and dependent Russia. China, once the confident champion of the Third World, is in a reserved and cautious mood. The Non-Aligned Movement (NAM), whose raison-d'être derived largely from the logic of East-West conflict, is in a state of political disorientation, searching for a new vocation in a rearranged world situation. The United States, despite its financial constraints and domestic preoccupation, has been thrust into a position of preeminence without a counterweight. Meanwhile, Germany and Japan have come into their own as world economic giants, now in search of appropriate global political roles.

With these developments, power relations in the Security Council have swung from one extreme to another. During the Cold War, East-

West and North-South cleavages provided a rigid and unproductive system of checks-and-balances. In the aftermath of the Cold War, as others have descended on the power ladder, the clout of the United States, supported by the other two Western permanent members, Britain and France, has increased enormously.

Thirdly, we are witnessing the emergence of a global community of values in relation to issues of human rights, democracy and humanitarian assistance. Even though some aspects of this development remain highly contentious, these values are increasingly providing impetus for collective international action. A credible international system for keeping the peace cannot function in a normative vacuum; it needs to be underpinned by a community of values.

These developments—the renewed authority of the Security Council, the realignment of power within the Security Council, and the emergence of a community of values—have brought to the fore an emerging concern: how to ensure that the decisions of the Security Council correspond to a broadly representative and global view of UN mandate on key questions of international peace and security? This is the challenge of maintaining broad-based and universal legitimacy for UN actions in the post-Cold War world. This chapter will discuss some of these "legitimacy" issues. Although the UN may not be facing a serious legitimacy crisis at the moment, there is a growing disquiet about the scope, nature and pace of Security Council decisions, as well as the process of decision-making. Whether the UN continues to command broad-based legitimacy will depend on how these and related issues are addressed in the long term.

A. ROLE OF THE SECURITY COUNCIL

With the traumatic experience of World War II still fresh in mind, the UN was founded with the ambition "to save succeeding generations from the scourge of war." The principal mandate of the new organization was to be the maintenance of international peace and security, for which primary responsibility was assigned to the Security Council.

Now that the Security Council has been freed from the Cold War gridlock, it has gained authority and effectiveness; so much so that some of its recent decisions have been breathtaking. Several issues of legitimacy arise in relation to the role and functioning of the Security Council.

1. Scope of the Mandate

First, there is the question of the scope of the Security Council's jurisdiction. The Security Council's mandate is to assume primary responsibility for the maintenance of international peace and security. In the past, the notion of "a threat to international peace and security" was generally understood to encompass an act of aggression or a breach of the peace, involving some actual or potential military manifestation, usually in the context of an inter-state or regional conflict.

In recent decisions of the Security Council, a trend is emerging of a more expansive interpretation of "a threat to international peace and security" by the Security Council. Measures being adopted have become increasingly intrusive and coercive, most of them aimed not so much at inter-state conflicts but at situations of internal strife.

Following the expulsion of Iraq from Kuwait, the Security Council, in Resolution 687 of March 1991, placed Iraq under the most comprehensive set of restrictions ever imposed on a country by the UN. The measures included: inspections to uncover and destroy proscribed weapons of mass destruction and long-term monitoring of weapons-related programs; enforced establishment of an observer force on the Iraqi/Kuwaiti border; enforced demarcation of the border between Iraq and Kuwait; determination of the level of war reparations to be paid out of Iraqi oil revenues; and a stipulation that the lifting of sanctions would depend on the "policies and practices of the (Iraqi) government." Later, in Resolution 688 of April 1991, the Security Council held that the internal repression of Iraqi civilian population, including the cross-border flow of refugees, threatened "international peace and security in the region."

In resolution 748 of March 1992, the Security Council made a determination that the failure of the Libyan government to extradite the suspects in the bombing of the Pan American jetliner that exploded over Lockerbie in Scotland in 1988 constituted a threat to international peace and security. In the case of Somalia, the Security Council in Resolution 794 of December 1992 determined that the "magnitude of human tragedy caused by the conflict in Somalia, ... constitut(ed) a threat to international peace and security."

Regardless of the particular circumstances that may have animated these decisions, they inevitably form a body of precedents; their far-reaching implications will be difficult to ignore in other situations in the future. Yet it is open to argument whether all these determinations fall truly within the scope of "a threat to international peace and security" as originally envisaged in the Charter of the UN.

Under Article 39 of the Charter a "threat to the peace" and a "breach of the peace" are among the specific conditions that can trigger action by the Security Council. These conditions were understood to refer primarily to situations of inter-state conflicts. This interpretation has been overtaken by events. The realities of the 1990s do not correspond to the very different world of 1945, when these concepts were incorporated in the Charter. In the immediate aftermath of World War II the dominant anxiety was understandably over threats of inter-state aggression; this concern therefore translated into the central mandate of the Security Council. By contrast, the preoccupation of the international community today is with the rampant breakdown of peace and security within national borders.

If the Security Council is to remain relevant, it must adapt to this evolving world situation. This means above all finding innovative ways to respond to situations of intra-state conflict. It also means developing a more progressive interpretation of "a threat to international peace and security" and "breach of the peace." In doing so, however, the Security Council should seek to build broad-based international consensus around its decisions. Intervention in Somalia gained legitimacy because it was able to command broad international support. On the other hand, the Security Council's determination that Libya's failure to extradite the suspects in the Lockerbie affair constituted a threat to international peace and security has remained controversial.

While the Security Council is self-regulating (a finding of a threat to the peace by the Security Council cannot be challenged) and in that sense can designate any development a "threat to the peace" or a "breach of the peace," the legitimacy and authority of that body could be eroded if it was seen as departing too far from the spirit of the Charter and a sense of international consensus. The situation calls for a judicious blend of political self-restraint on the one hand and progressive interpretation of Charter provisions on the other.

2. Decision-Making Process

Questions about decision-making in the Security Council have been compounded by a practice which has developed in recent times, tending towards *less* transparency and *less* participation. This method of work has been vividly described by Professor Michael Reisman:[1]

> Magnifying the disquiet is the fact that, as the Council has become more effective and powerful, it has become more secretive. Like a parliamentary matryoskhka (doll), it now contains ever-smaller "mini-

Councils," each meeting behind closed doors without keeping records, and each taking decisions secretly. Before the plenary Council meets in "consultation," in a special room assigned to it near the Security Council, the P-5 have met in "consultation" in a special room now assigned to them outside the Security Council; and before they meet, the P-3 composed of the United States, the United Kingdom and France, have met in "consultation" in one of their missions in New York. All of these meetings take place *in camera* and no common minutes are kept. After the fifteen members of the Council have consulted and reached their decision, they adjourn to the Council's chamber, where they go through the formal motions of voting and announcing their decision. Decisions that appear to go further than at any time in the history of the United Nations are now ultimately being taken, it seems, by a small group of states separately meeting in secret.

In view of the increasingly far-reaching character of measures being adopted by the Council, there is a growing demand on the part of the wider UN membership to be associated more closely with the making of decisions. Indeed, the Security Council is not meant to function in isolation. After all, the legitimacy of the Security Council derives from the special responsibility *conferred* upon it by the membership of the UN as a whole; thus the 15 members of the Security Council act on behalf of the entire 183 members of the organization.[2] It is in this context that the Charter assigns to the Security Council primary but *not exclusive* responsibility for the maintenance of international peace and security.

The challenge is to develop a practice which responds to the need for more transparency and greater participation, while at the same time ensuring prompt and effective action. One way to reduce this sense of exclusion would be for the Security Council to adopt a two-track approach in its proceedings. In addition to the informal consultations, which are private and held behind closed doors, the Security Council should make it a practice to schedule more public sessions before making final decisions on important questions, such as the use of collective force for enforcement action, the imposition of sanctions, or undertaking a major peacekeeping operation. The open sessions would serve as a form of "public hearings," giving the wider UN membership the opportunity to make their inputs on important questions that ultimately affect them. Decisions of the Security Council would then emerge following both informal behind-the-scenes consultations and public discussions. Such a practice would not entail any modifications in existing rules of procedure.

Another way to improve communication between the Security Council and the rest of the UN membership would be for the non-permanent members, who are after all elected on a regional basis, to hold regular briefing sessions for their respective regional groups. Some of this is going on now on an ad hoc basis, depending on the initiatives of individual members of the Security Council. This needs to be developed into an institutional practice for all regional groups.

Finally, the Security Council should institute a system of regular consultations with countries that may be particularly affected by measures under consideration. Such groups might consist of troop-contributing countries, third countries likely to be affected by sanctions measures or concerned neighboring states when a situation within a country is under discussion in the Security Council.

3. Toward Recomposition?

Another issue of legitimacy for the Security Council concerns its present composition, consisting of five permanent members and ten non-permanent members chosen on a regional basis. This membership structure essentially reflects the world situation of 1945 when, in the aftermath of World War II, the principal Allied powers and China assumed permanent seats with the veto right. The realignment of power since then, together with the growth in UN membership (from 51 in 1945 to 183 in 1993) are producing strong pressure for the recomposition of the Security Council. Japan's bid for a permanent seat and a similar if less aggressive claim by Germany, as well as the long-standing claims of several developing countries, have given a strong thrust to the movement for change.

It is now clear that a reform of the Security Council cannot be postponed indefinitely. However, the challenge of coming up with a formula and timetable for recomposition that can command broad concurrence remains formidable. The process of consensus-building on this issue should begin right away with the goal of reaching a consensus formula by 1995, the fiftieth anniversary year for the UN.

The following is a scenario that could constitute a basis for restructuring the Security Council. The new Security Council would have a three-tier membership structure. The first tier would consist of the present permanent members: China, France, Russia, the United Kingdom, the United States. They would retain their right of veto, but with the understanding that the veto would be used in the more restrictive spirit envisaged in the Charter. The veto should be a defense mechanism to be used *in extremis*, a kind of shield to protect a permanent member when its vital national interest is at stake. This would be a departure from the trigger-happy use of the veto that became the hallmark of the Security Council during the Cold War. Already in the last few years public opinion in the UN has turned against the permissive use of the veto. The burden of responsibility for invoking the veto has increased. Indeed since May 1990 no veto has been cast in the Security Council.[3]

The second tier of membership would be composed of new permanent members without the right of veto. Japan and Germany would certainly qualify for this, but it would be difficult to grant permanent seats to Japan and Germany without making a similar dispensation for some of the developing countries with strong and long-standing claims. In addition to Japan and Germany therefore, there would be three other new permanent members chosen on a regional basis. The strongest candidates are: Brazil representing Latin America and the Caribbean, India representing Asia and Nigeria representing Africa. Alternatively as an interim measure, pending long-term review, each of the new five might be given a fixed term of ten years with eligibility for re-election.

The third tier would consist of rotating non-permanent members, in the same way as at present. This category would be marginally expanded from ten to eleven seats. This would bring the total membership of the new Security Council to twenty-one. This is a manageable size that assures greater representation while preserving the need for prompt and effective action by the Security Council.[4]

As part of the reorganization of the Security Council an additional measure needs to be considered, namely the creation of the right of regional veto. Initially this veto could be granted to the two regions where no veto power presently exists:[5] Latin America and Africa. However, through a progressive review process the same arrangements could be extended to other regions in the future. A regional veto is necessarily a collective defense mechanism to be invoked only when a fundamental regional interest is at stake. Such a veto would be exercised upon the unanimous agreement of the Security Council members of the region concerned.

Finally, whatever the outcome of the proposed review the composition of the Security Council should not be set in stone. It is necessary to review the situation on a periodic basis, preferably every ten years, in order to take into account the evolution of power relations in the world.

B. INTERVENTION AND LEGITIMACY

Recent developments have dramatized the whole question of intervention by the UN on account of grave humanitarian and human rights developments within a given country. The question is: when is intervention permissible and can this be reconciled with what has hitherto been viewed as a pillar of the international system, namely the principle of non-interference in the internal affairs of states, enshrined in Article 2.7 of the Charter?

As things now stand, Article 2.7 constitutes a powerful but not an absolute barrier against "intervention" or "involvement" by the international community. Consider the following situations where some form of "intervention" by the UN is now considered admissible:

- collective action under Chapter VII. This is an explicit exception.

- when the state concerned gives its consent to the involvement of the UN in matters otherwise within the state's domestic jurisdiction. Examples of this include the monitoring of elections in various countries, the mediation exercise by the Secretary-General in El Salvador, and present efforts to monitor peace accords in Angola and Mozambique.

- when an internal conflict has assumed a major international dimension and when this fact is recognized as such by the internal factions as well as their external sponsors. The present situation in Cambodia; the situation in Afghanistan before the withdrawal of Soviet troops; and the negotiations that led to the withdrawal of South African and Cuban troops from Angola belong to this category of UN intervention.

- denunciation of human rights abuses in a given country by the UN Commission on Human Rights or the General Assembly. It is rare nowadays for a government to simply say, "you have no right to express concern about the human rights situation within my borders." A government under attack is more likely to argue that: "the facts you allege are not correct"; "you are selective in expressing your concerns"; or that "the real reason for your denunciation is not concern for human rights but a hidden political agenda."

In the scenarios cited above, intervention seems acceptable, if not always welcome. These are the "easy cases." But how should we answer the question which is at the heart of the present debate: in what circumstances is *forcible intervention* acceptable in response to a grave humanitarian and human rights situation within a country? Unlike the examples given above, this type of intervention involves the forcible insertion of UN presence, often military, in a country without the consent of the authorities concerned. The various types of intervention in this category represent in effect the "hard cases."

Two schools of thought have rapidly emerged within the UN on this issue. The one is the *activist school* that seeks a more flexible interpretation of Article 2.7. The other is the *status quo school* that is deeply suspicious of any further erosion of the barrier erected in Article 2.7. It should be noted that this debate has increasingly taken on a North-South dimension, with the leading industrialized countries belonging to the activist school while most developing countries tend to favor the alternative approach.

There are two competing principles here that will need to be balanced over time. On the one hand, the stability of the inter-state system depends on accepting and respecting the sovereign rights of states. On the other hand, there is a major evolution in thinking at the level of international public opinion that can no longer accept that massive and dramatic suffering should be shielded behind the walls of sovereignty. In effect, the notion of what constitutes the "domestic affairs" of a state is undergoing some change.

The search is for a threshold, an acceptable threshold. When, and in what circumstances, is the level of suffering within a given country of such magnitude as to warrant forcible intervention by the international community?

It is unlikely that the search for an appropriate threshold will be resolved by a juridical design. The appropriate threshold is more likely to emerge slowly over a period of time, on a case-by-case basis. Yet, a case-by-case approach must not lead to major inconsistencies. It is therefore necessary over time to develop a broad framework of considerations to guide the evolution of practice. These parameters might fall into three categories: basic prerequisites for intervention, emerging areas of consensus, and the issue of feasibility.

1. Basic Prerequisites for Intervention

From the outset, there are three basic prerequisites that need to be satisfied before the Security Council considers the option of intervening in an internal situation. First, it should be a situation of massive and systematic suffering, whether arising from natural (famine) or human (war) causes. Second, the situation must be such that it can elicit a strong response for action from a wide spectrum of the international community. Finally, since intervention by the Security Council is necessarily a radical step, it should be a measure of last resort, to be applied only when all other remedies or means of pressure have been exhausted. Such means of peaceful pressure can include: action by the General Assembly or the UN Commission on Human Rights; initiatives by regional organizations; use of the good-offices of the Secretary-General; as well as bilateral diplomatic pressure exercised by those well-placed to influence the course of events in a given situation. The situations in Bosnia-Herzegovina, Somalia, Liberia and to some extent Iraq have certainly satisfied the basic prerequisites set out above.

2. Emerging Consensus Scenarios for Intervention

In recent decisions of the Security Council some tentative trends are beginning to emerge concerning intervention. Essentially there are four scenarios around which consensus is likely to evolve in the future.

The first scenario involves intervention to provide access for relief assistance to populations in distress. Typically this entails the opening of routes blocked by parties in conflict and the escort of relief convoys to target populations. This then is intervention to provide *military protection of humanitarian relief*. Recent examples of this type of intervention include operations in northern Iraq, Somalia, and Bosnia-Herzegovina. Resolution 688 of April 1991, concerning the situation of the Kurds in Northern Iraq, was the first step in this direction. Here, massive internal repression and the flow of refugees across international borders became grounds for the three Western permanent members of the Security Council to intervene to protect the Kurdish populations. While the Security Council never formally endorsed the intervention, it insisted "that Iraq allow immediate access by international humanitarian organizations to all those in need of assistance in all parts of Iraq and to make available all necessary facilities for their operations." Later UN guards were deployed, with the consent of the Iraqi authorities, to monitor humanitarian relief efforts.

The deteriorating situation in Bosnia-Herzegovina, the attacks on relief convoys and the general obstruction of humanitarian assistance by the warring factions resulted in the adoption of resolution 770 in August 1992. The Security Council, acting under Chapter VII of the Charter, called on States to "take nationally or through regional agencies or arrangements all measures necessary to facilitate, in coordination with the UN, the delivery of humanitarian assistance to Sarajevo and wherever needed in other parts of Bosnia-Herzegovina."

An even more radical development was the decision on Somalia in December 1992, when the Security Council in resolution 794 specifically "authorize(d) the Secretary-General and Member States...to use all necessary means to establish as soon as possible a secure environment for humanitarian relief operations." The situation in Somalia by this time was one of generalized violence, where the state had already collapsed. Consequently, humanitarian relief was hampered not only by the civil strife ravaging the country, but also by the obstruction of relief workers who were being subjected to extortion, blackmail and robbery.

The second scenario involves intervention to provide direct *military protection to populations under siege*. This means placing designated areas, so-called safe-areas or safe-havens, under the direct responsibility of the UN. In addition, the recent practice of declaring "no-fly zones" in conflict areas also falls under this category. In northern Iraq, relying on the authority of resolution 688, the Western powers established a safe-haven for Kurds which is now being monitored by 500 UN guards with the consent of the Iraqi authorities. The same Western powers also established, under the authority of resolution 688, a "no-fly zone" which calls for the end to the repression of the Kurds in northern Iraq and the Shiites in the south. This "air exclusion zone" has had the tacit approval of the Security Council.

The Security Council has in recent resolutions (resolution 819 in April 1993 and resolution 824 in May 1993) concerning the situation in the former Yugoslavia established "safe areas" which should be free from any armed or hostile attacks and to which the United Nations Protection Force (UNPROFOR) and international humanitarian agencies should be allowed free and unimpeded access. A "no-fly zone" was established by the Security Council in October 1992, prior to the demarcation of "safe-havens," which banned all military flights in the air space of Bosnia-Herzegovina. Violations of the "no-fly zone" in March 1993 resulted in the adoption of resolution 816 which authorized Member States to take "all necessary measures" in the airspace of Bosnia and Herzegovina to ensure compliance with the ban on flights.[6]

The third scenario would involve intervention to enforce a peace accord or a cease-fire agreement. This means applying "forceful persuasion" or a measure of compulsion if necessary to ensure that parties to an agreement abide by their commitments. It may also be employed to ensure that minor parties (not under the direct control of any signatories to the agreement) do no sabotage the peace process. This mode of operation would be quite different from the more passive traditional peacekeeping role which was merely to monitor the implementation of agreements. The traditional mode has worked well in the context of inter-state agreements, but has proven ineffective in the more convoluted situations of civil wars. The idea here is that a significant and forceful military presence by the UN would make it more difficult for parties to renege on their commitments or sabotage the implementation of agreements. This might be called *enforcement monitoring of agreements.*

Any eventual peace accord on Bosnia-Herzegovina would almost certainly require enforcement monitoring by the UN. The peace process in Angola might not have broken down so tragically if there had been a major and forceful UN military presence. In Cambodia, the Khmer Rouge have declined to participate in the recent elections. But if they had proceeded beyond that to an active sabotage of the entire peace process, the Security Council might have had to consider forceful means to curtail their activities and save the Paris Agreements.

The last scenario is of *intervention to re-build a collapsed state*. This takes place in a situation where the central authority or the state has effectively collapsed leaving in its wake a state of generalized violence among warring factions. Today, Somalia and Liberia best exemplify this type of situation. But there are other states, mainly in Africa and the former Soviet Union, which have become so fragile that they could well suffer the same fate.

Intervention by the UN in a country where the state has collapsed is a particularly radical and ambitious undertaking. The scope of such intervention must necessarily be broad, encompassing the restoration of an environment of security, disarming of the factions, the establishment of an integrated army, organizing elections, establishing a framework for national reconciliation and resurrecting defunct state structures such as the judiciary, the police or the civil service. These are new and particularly daunting departures in UN engagements.

3. Issue of Feasibility

When considering intervention, the Security Council should take into account not only what is *permissible* under the Charter but also what is *feasible* at the practical level, given the limited capacity of the UN.

The last few years have seen an escalation of demands for UN intervention, mostly in the convoluted situations of internal conflicts, requiring complex and novel operations. Since 1989 the UN has established fifteen new operations, (which contrasts with the fourteen instituted in the previous 41 years), deploying over 90,000 military, police and civilian personnel at an annualized cost that reached $4 billion in 1993. Of these operations fourteen are currently under way. These commitments have already stretched to the limit the capacity of the UN for effective response. And demands continue to mount.

This is in part the result of overblown expectations about the capacity of the organization. But it is also in no small measure due to the fact that there is nowhere else to go! With the end of the Cold War the "godfathers" who sponsored as well as contained many of those conflicts have gone home. And at the level of regional organizations, local efforts have not yet produced viable mechanisms for managing conflicts.

Meanwhile at the UN, the gap between expectations and realities is growing ever wider. Unless member states are prepared to equip the UN with much stronger organizational and military capabilities as well as the necessary financial resources, the organization will not be able to respond effectively to the new peace-and-security challenges being thrust upon it. Indeed without strengthening its capacity, UN performance even on present commitments is likely to suffer and with it the credibility of the organization.

In the meantime as a practical matter, the Security Council may have to adopt a policy of selective engagement concerning further demands for intervention. This would mean choosing more carefully where and when to intervene, and concentrating on conflict situations where the insertion of the UN can be effective and make a significant difference. While selective engagement is perhaps a necessary response to present realities, it has serious drawbacks as a long-term policy. Under selective engagement, conflicts will fall into two categories: those "adopted" by the UN and the ones that are allowed to fall between the cracks of the international system. The latter will comprise conflicts which have been abandoned either because they are too complex or because they are too many. These conflicts will be left to run their own course and would effectively constitute the "forgotten tragedies" of the world. This presents a serious moral dilemma. The answer may well lie in pursuing a policy of selective engagement as a short-term measure, while mobilizing resources to strengthen the capability of the UN as well as that of regional organizations. This also underscores the critical importance for the UN and regional organizations to make preventive action an arena of particular priority, thus responding at the preventive and earlier stages of conflict.

C. LEGITIMACY AND SANCTIONS

The issue of the legitimacy of economic sanctions is not new, but has been highlighted by the recent experience during the Gulf Crisis. The sanctions measures enacted against Iraq after the invasion and annexation of Kuwait were by far the most comprehensive ever put into place by the UN. Yet they were eventually considered inadequate for the task of reversing Iraq's aggression against Kuwait. Since then the Security Council has imposed sanctions against Serbia and Libya, and Haiti.

In considering the effectiveness of any given sanctions régime, we need to bear in mind two distinct but related aspects. First, to what extent are sanctions measures successful in isolating the target country? This may be called *physical effectiveness*, which will depend on the scope of the sanctions in place as well as the extent of their observance by the wider international community. The second aspect of effectiveness is more complex and very difficult to measure: to what extent are sanctions likely to *induce* the necessary change of policy or attitude on the part of the target government? This is *political effectiveness*, which is likely to depend on certain particularities of the target country, including for example, the willingness of its government to enforce massive and prolonged hardship on the population and, we should not forget, the sheer determination of a state, for whatever reasons, to pursue a chosen policy almost regardless of the cost involved.

Closely related to the question of effectiveness is the issue of time frame and scope of the sanctions régime imposed. What is a reasonable time frame within which to judge the effectiveness of sanctions in a given situation? If it is possible to have a sense of what constitutes a reasonable time frame, it may be useful to indicate this from the outset, perhaps by inscribing it in the resolution enacting the sanctions measures. There also needs to be a greater clarity with respect to the objectives.

Another problem relating to sanctions is the nefarious impact of sanctions on other countries. We live in a world that, more than ever before, is characterized by deep linkages among the economies of many countries. The Gulf Crisis demonstrated that when these links have to be severed abruptly, the impact can be devastating, especially for the weaker economies of developing countries. It became clear during the Gulf Crisis that, in spite of the provision of Article 50 of the Charter, no concrete framework has in fact been developed for providing assistance to countries seriously affected by the application of sanctions. An unprecedented number of countries (21 in all) applied for assistance from the Security Council under Article 50 in 1991, each claiming billions of dollars worth of losses. In order to encourage future compliance with sanctions régimes, it is important that this problem be addressed in a more systematic and satisfactory manner. Similarly, the Security Council needs to address the problem of humanitarian consequences of sanctions, especially on civilian populations within target countries.

The last sanctions issue concerns the manner of determining the adequacy or inadequacy of sanctions measures. Article 42 of the Charter provides that the Security Council shall first determine that sanctions measures "would be inadequate or have proved to be inadequate" before resorting to the use of force. However, it is not clear how this is to be done. Here too there is need for reflection and clarification with regard to future action.

It would be useful for the Security Council to review how this particular weapon—sanctions—may be used in the future. Such a review could be conducted by a committee of the Security Council or alternatively that organ could appoint an independent commission of experts drawn from the membership of the Security Council.

D. ROLE OF THE SECRETARY-GENERAL

Managing the peace-and-security agenda of the UN depends on the Security Council and the Secretary-General working closely together. This involves a special and often delicate relationship. In general, the Security Council tends to intervene when a situation has reached a stage requiring some formal action. The Secretary-General, on the other hand, is more effective in situations requiring informal, flexible, and often discreet initiatives, some of which may pave the way for more formal action by the Security Council.

This relationship is evolving. At the Security Council summit in January 1992, the idea of an enhanced role for the Secretary-General, especially in the areas of preventive diplomacy and peacemaking, seemed to gain wide support. Moreover in the public mind, a sense of legitimacy for the UN is closely associated with the role of the

Secretary-General. He is "Mr. United Nations," a symbol of the collectivity of the organization. He alone stands above the expression of national and regional interests that are often competing for dominance within the organization. He can plead for a sense of balance and a universal perspective, when this is in danger of being lost. It was in this spirit that last year, Dr. Boutros Boutros-Ghali expressed his urgent concern to the Security Council when he felt that it had become too preoccupied with Yugoslavia and not sufficiently engaged on Somalia.

In a more formal way, the Charter provides in Article 99 for the Secretary-General, when he deems it necessary, to bring to the attention of the Security Council any developments that may threaten international peace and security. This article has rarely been used. Indeed, for the most part, it may not be necessary for the Secretary-General to formally invoke Article 99; he can, on an informal basis, bring any serious developments to the attention of the Security Council. However, when he deems it useful, there is the option of invoking Article 99 as a formal alarm bell.

The international community looks to the Secretary-General to provide important diplomatic and intellectual leadership. He can only play that role when there is strong support and encouragement from the Security Council, especially on the part of the five permanent members.

E. PUBLIC PERCEPTION

An important aspect of the issue of legitimacy for the UN is the question of international public perception, especially with regard to the collective use of force by the UN. The public perception of the UN is largely dependent on the effectiveness of the organization in the sphere of intervention and enforcement action. The authorization of the use of force by the Security Council in the Gulf War, for example, produced very contradictory reactions, especially within two particular constituencies. On one side, what may be called the traditional UN constituency seemed somewhat dismayed and disoriented, finding it difficult to accept the fact that the UN could be the instrument of waging war, even if that war was aimed at rolling back aggression and even though it was authorized under Chapter VII of the Charter. The other constituency consists of those who had hitherto tended to view the UN skeptically as a soft option, a mere talking shop which could not be entrusted with the more serious business of repelling aggression.

This group was pleasantly surprised. It rallied and enthused. The UN could act with resolve and dispatch, after all.

The fact is that the UN needs both constituencies. The challenge is to build a bridge between these two apparently divergent views. Clearly the UN cannot operate solely on the basis of ideals and principles, divorced from the realities of the world of power politics. This would render it a utopian project. On the other hand, the UN cannot simply mirror the world of *realpolitik*. The UN should be the place where power relations are recognized but mediated by ideals and principles. It is this unique blend which can give the UN legitimacy on a universal plane.

NOTES

1. W. Michael Reisman, "The Constitutional Crisis in the United Nations," *American Journal of International Law* 87:1 (January 1993), pp. 85-86. Prof. Reisman cites Anthony Aust, "The Procedure and Practice of the Security Council Today" (unpublished manuscript).
2. See Article 24(1) of the UN Charter.
3. The exception was the May 1993 Russian veto on the mandatory financing for the UN Peacekeeping Force in Cyprus. It has been acknowledged that the Russian decision to veto the resolution was taken out of practical and not political considerations.
4. Under this scenario the passage of a resolution would require the affirmative vote of thirteen members (including the concurring votes of the permanent members) which would maintain the proportionality of the voting requirements that exists today.
5. In the current distribution of the veto power on a regional basis, Asia has one (China), Europe has three (Britain, France, and now Russia) and North America has one (United States of America).
6. Security Council Resolution 816 (1993) specifically *"authorizes* Member States, seven days after the adoption of this resolution, acting nationally or through regional organizations or arrangements, to take, under the authority of the Security Council and subject to close coordination with the Secretary-General and UNPROFOR, all necessary measures in the airspace of the Republic of Bosnia and Herzegovina, in the event of further violations, to ensure compliance with the ban on flights referred to in paragraph 1 above, and proportionate to the specific circumstances and the nature of the flights...."

VI. SUMMARY OF RECOMMENDATIONS

We noted at the outset that some current multilateral peacekeeping operations are faltering. This report has not addressed the complex political choices to be made in particular cases. We have addressed systemic improvements in multilateral peacekeeping which these and other cases have indicated are necessary (if not sufficient) for success over time, in what is a critical area for Trilateral countries in shaping a constructive post-Cold War era. The issues are not just those arising from particular conflict situations; they are related to the kind of world—the kind of international leadership and cooperation—that will follow the Cold War era.

In his chapter, John Roper, after noting the expansion of United Nations tasks in the framework of a revived Security Council, describes the major adaptation underway of regional organizations centered on Europe. NATO, WEU and the EC are acting in direct cooperation with the United Nations to implement Security Council resolutions in ex-Yugoslavia. Roper points to the eventual possibility of a formal agreement between WEU or NATO and the United Nations on the availability of forces, under Article 43 of Charter. (Masashi Nishihara suggests in his later chapter that similar missions may be added to Japan-U.S. security arrangements, under a United Nations mandate.) This adaptation of Europe-centered organizations will help in the case of future European crises, but Roper cautions against thereby weakening UN capabilities in other regions—and his primary recommendations concern improving arrangements for deploying United Nations forces.

Roper recommends planning for three levels of UN forces. At the first level, the United Nations should have at its disposal a highly trained standing ready force of four or five battalions (600-700 troops each) drawn from one or two nations and trained to operate as a single unit. Such a force could be used quickly for preventive deployments or as the advance guard of a more substantial force. At the second level, the United Nations should have rapid deployment forces from the armed forces of member states which could be deployed at very few days' notice. If ten countries or groups of countries were each prepared to provide a brigade group (about 5,000 troops each), the UN could deploy forces of up to 50,000 men. Such rapid deployment forces would enable the Security Council to respond early to a conflict or potential conflict situation. The very availability of such a capacity at the disposal of the international community could have a deterrent effect. At the third level, in a case of serious aggression by a regional power (such as Iraq against Kuwait in 1990), it would be necessary to assemble a coalition of more substantial forces. Even at this level, troops could be earmarked for such purposes and receive appropriate training. At all three levels, improvements will have to be made in UN headquarters capabilities and command structures, which sometimes can be supplied by regional arrangements (as by NATO for UNPROFOR 2).

Enid Schoettle makes clear in her chapter that a continuing financial crisis is paralyzing the UN's ability to carry out its rapidly expanding activities. Unless these financial problems are resolved and more reliable financial mechanisms put in place, the United Nations will not be able to play the new role which governments—particularly Trilateral governments—claim they want it to play. UN peacekeeping is growing rapidly, and thus so are its costs, at a time of declining defense and international affairs budgets in Trilateral countries, but these costs are not unmanageable in comparison with what governments ordinarily consider as normal defense expenditures. Trilateral governments need to recognize that UN peacekeeping is now a central, ongoing mission for their national security, and be prepared to fund it accordingly.

Schoettle divides her recommendations into two parts. The first are for Trilateral governments and regional organizations to which they belong:

- The single greatest contribution to solving the UN's problems in financing peacekeeping would be for Trilateral governments to *pay assessments in full and on time*. The stark fact is that these are legal obligations. Above all this is a challenge for the United States.

- The *shifting of expenditure responsibility for UN peacekeeping to Defense Ministries* would make sense in a number of Trilateral countries. In other countries, the solution may be different. There is much to be said for a peacekeeping contingency fund at the Presidential or Prime-Ministerial level.

- The Secretary-General is requesting governments to *earmark standby capabilities of all sorts for rapid assignment to the UN.* Now is the time for Trilateral governments to respond.

- It is important at this juncture for all governments *to reiterate the principle of collective financial responsibility for UN peacekeeping.* Within this framework, however, there must be provision for ad hoc adjustments, for substantial *voluntary contributions* from countries which can afford them.

Schoettle's second set of recommendations are for Trilateral countries to urge on the United Nations:

- To streamline the now almost incessant flow of assessments for separate peacekeeping operations, the UN should *adopt a single annual budget for peacekeeping,* as the Ogata-Volcker report suggested. *Increases are needed in reserves*—the Working Capital Fund and the Peacekeeping Reserve Fund.

- *The UN Secretariat needs to be able to plan and manage peacekeeping operations in a much more sophisticated manner.* The UN needs more resources of several types: (1) an operations center with real-time communications links to peacekeeping missions in the field; (2) strengthened planning, field operations and budgeting units within the Department of Peacekeeping Operations; (3) expanded peacekeeping training; and (4) expanded stockpiles.

- *The special peacekeeping scale of assessment,* fixed in 1973, needs to be revised and kept current.

- *Major changes need to be made in the administrative, personnel, and financial management practices at the UN.* An institution comparable to the U.S. General Accounting Office could regularly analyze ongoing UN operations and propose improvements.

- *Serious thinking needs to begin about new sources of UN financing,* other than assessed or voluntary government contributions.

Masashi Nishihara devotes most of his chapter to discussion of the challenges particular Trilateral countries face in enlarging national contributions to the strengthening of multilateral peacekeeping. He divides Trilateral countries into three categories:

- "Full-fledged traditional peacekeepers," such as Canada and a number of smaller countries in Europe, contributed significantly to UN peacekeeping during the Cold War by monitoring ceasefires and separating combatants. With the emergence of a new, more uncertain era, most of these Trilateral countries are willing to contribute even more, but sending troops into multiple operations in risky areas raises new and difficult issues of interests, resources, and options.

- Germany and Japan—"self-restrained peacekeepers"—are particularly important as two large countries whose capabilities have been underused for multilateral peacekeeping efforts. The Constitutional Court has helped resolve aspects of the constitutional issue in Germany. There is no constitutional court in Japan, where it may be more realistic, Nishihara argues, to give a more flexible interpretation to the constitution rather than to try to revise it. Suspicion in Asian countries about Japan's participation in UN peacekeeping operations seems to be fading away since a Japanese contingent started its mission in Cambodia in 1992. Likewise, international opinion toward Germany has changed drastically.

- The United States, France, and the United Kingdom are the primary "peace-enforcers." The Americans have to sort out to what extent they are willing to place their forces under a non-American commander. The Clinton Administration also has the important task of linking America's lift, communications, logistics, and intelligence capabilities to an enhanced UN role. Will the United States continue to be willing to play the role of catalyst for large-scale military operations? France and Britain enjoy their reputations as responsible permanent members of the UN Security Council with dangerous peace-enforcing roles, but they feel their resources and capabilities are being stretched virtually to the limit.

Nishihara concludes his paper with a number of recommendations for Trilateral cooperation in making multilateral efforts more effective. The first four carry forward the third recommendation advanced by Schoettle:

- Agree on a target number of forces available for UN operations, and submit forces and their capabilities;

- With the above target in mind, explore and develop human and material resources fully for peacekeeping, peace-enforcing, and humanitarian operations;

- Promote efficient use of each other's capabilities; and

- Share training and exercise facilities.

Following up Roper's discussion of adding UN-sanctioned missions to regional security institutions centered in Europe, Nishihara proposes that the Japanese and Americans explore the possibility of jointly using resources that are under the Japan-U.S. Security Treaty for peacekeeping efforts under a UN mandate. Non-military materials needed for the swift introduction of UN civilian and military personnel into a new mission in Asia may be stockpiled at a base in Japan, for instance. An advance agreement in which Japanese troops can use American bases in Diego Garcia and other military facilities would greatly help Japan overcome its own severely limited lift capabilities in participating in distant UN peacekeeping operations. Finally, Nishihara stresses the need for Trilateral countries to develop dialogue with Russia and China, whose resources have remained seriously underutilized for multilateral peacekeeping efforts.

Olara Otunnu's chapter reminds us that broad legitimacy must be maintained in sufficient measure if the system of strengthened multilateral peacekeeping is to succeed over time. There is no legitimacy crisis at the moment, but there is a growing disquiet, Otunnu argues, about the scope, nature and pace of Security Council decisions, as well as the process of decision-making.

Are there any limits on the scope of the Council's competence? The Council is self-regulating and in that sense can designate any development "a threat to international peace and security." However, if the Council was seen as departing too far from the spirit of the Charter and a sense of international consensus, this could erode its authority and legitimacy. The situation calls for a judicious blend of political self-restraint on the one hand and progressive interpretation of Charter provisions on the other.

The new collegial atmosphere of the Council has increased the importance of informal discussions and thus decreased transparency—and sense of participation—for countries not represented. Otunnu recommends that the Council make it a practice to schedule more open sessions before making final decisions on important questions, such as the use of collective force for enforcement action, the imposition of sanctions, or undertaking a major peacekeeping operation. The open sessions would give the wider membership the opportunity to make their inputs on important questions that ultimately affect them. He also recommends that non-permanent members of the Council, already elected on a regional basis, hold regular briefing sessions with their respective regional groups.

The recomposition of the Security Council, Otunnu argues, cannot be postponed indefinitely. He recommends the new Council have a three-tier membership structure. The first tier would consist of the present permanent members, who would retain their right of veto, but with the understanding that the veto would be used in the more restrictive spirit envisaged in the Charter. The second tier would be composed of new permanent members without the right of veto: Brazil, India, Japan, Germany and Nigeria. The third tier would consist of rotating non-permanent members, in the same way as at present but marginally expanded from ten to eleven seats. The total membership of the Council would rise to 21. This is a manageable size, Otunnu argues, that assures greater representation while preserving the need for prompt and effective action by the Council.

Recent developments have dramatized the whole question of intervention by the United Nations on account of grave humanitarian and human rights developments within a country. In what circumstances is forcible intervention acceptable? On the one hand, Otunnu argues, the stability of the inter-state system depends on accepting and respecting the sovereign rights of states. On the other hand, there is a major evolution in thinking at the level of international public opinion that can no longer accept that massive and dramatic suffering should be shielded behind the walls of sovereignty. The search is for an acceptable threshold.

Otunnu suggests three basic prerequisites for intervention. First, it should be a situation of massive and systematic suffering. Second, the situation must be able to elicit a strong response for action from a wide spectrum of the international community. Third, intervention by the Security Council should be a last resort, applied only when all other means have been exhausted.

Four consensus scenarios for intervention are emerging, Otunnu argues. One is intervention to provide military protection of humanitarian relief. Second is intervention to provide direct military protection to populations under seige. Third is what Otunnu calls "enforcement monitoring of agreements." Fourth is intervention to rebuild a collapsed state.

As a practical matter, given the current limited capacity of the UN, the Security Council may have to adopt a policy of selective engagement concerning further demands for intervention. This has serious drawbacks as a long-term policy. The answer may lie in pursuing selective engagement as a short-term measure while mobilizing resources to strengthen the capability of the UN and regional organizations. This also underscores the critical importance of preventive action at earlier stages of conflict.

In the public mind, a sense of legitimacy for the United Nations is closely associated with the role of the Secretary-General. He can plead for a sense of balance and a universal perspective, when this is in danger of being lost. He can only play that role effectively, Otunnu emphasizes, when there is strong support and encouragement from the Security Council, especially on the part of the permanent members.

*　　　*　　　*

The communiqué from the G-7 London Summit in July 1991 declared:

> We believe the conditions now exist for the United Nations to fulfill completely the promise and vision of its founders. A revitalized United Nations will have a central role in strengthening the international order. We commit ourselves to making the UN stronger, more efficient and more effective in order to protect human rights, to maintain peace and security for all and to deter aggression. We will make preventive diplomacy a top priority to help avert future conflicts by making clear to potential aggressors the consequences of their actions. The UN's role in peace-keeping should be reinforced and we are prepared to do this strongly.[1]

Similar declarations emerged from the UN Security Council Summit in January 1992, the Munich Summit in July 1992, and the Tokyo Summit in July 1993. Making a reality of this commitment to strengthened multilateral peacekeeping is a process to which this report is intended to contribute.

NOTE

1. As quoted in Richard N. Gardner, "The Role of the United Nations in Collective Security," *Working Group Papers 1991-92* (New York: Trilateral Commission, 1992)

APPENDIX

The following speech by Marrack Goulding was given on March 28, 1993, at the annual meeting of the Trilateral Commission—just before consideration of a draft of the report printed above. The Goulding remarks are themselves an important contribution to the current debate and we are pleased to present them as an appendix to this report. Marrack Goulding is United Nations Under-Secretary-General for Political Affairs. He was Under-Secretary-General for Peacekeeping Operations until early 1993. Some of the ideas in this speech he developed in more detail in the Cyril Foster Lecture delivered at Oxford University in early March, a lecture printed in the July 1993 issue of International Affairs, *the quarterly journal of the Royal Institute of International Affairs (Chatham House). Like that lecture, the speech that follows was a statement of his personal views and not an official statement of the United Nations Secretary General's position.*

CURRENT RAPID EXPANSION UNSUSTAINABLE WITHOUT MAJOR CHANGES

Marrack Goulding

The authors of the report have presented the meeting with four remarkable contributions—accurate, up-to-date, full of insight, and full of valuable ideas—and they provide an excellent basis for discussion this morning. When I read them I was left with the feeling that there wasn't a great deal for the visiting speaker to say. I propose to do two things. The first is to offer a classification or typology of peacekeeping, as it has evolved in recent years. There has been a tendency—to some extent reflected in the draft report—to speak of peacekeeping as though it is a homogeneous or monotypic activity. That is not, in fact, the case. A brief analysis of the different types of peacekeeping will show what a varied activity it has become, and how rapidly it is evolving.

Secondly, I would like to discuss some of the less positive consequences of the very rapid expansion which has taken place in peacekeeping, and certain steps which need to be taken to make sure that those less than happy consequences don't undermine the whole activity. The Secretary-General's position today is a bit like that of a producer of consumer goods who has faced a very welcome, but massive and somewhat unexpected, increase in demand for his product—his product being peacekeeping. He has done everything possible to respond to that demand. He has increased production, established new outlets, hired extra staff. But the reality, which has become very clear during 1992, is that he does not have the managerial or financial structures to sustain for very long this highly increased rate of production. Unless this is quickly put right, things may go wrong, the quality of the product may decline, the necessary finance will not be available, and he will run the danger of losing control to the bankers, the consultants, the rival entrepreneurs, who all seem to be wanting to help but may have agendas of their own

*   *   *

There have been two broad phases in the evolution of peacekeeping. There was the Cold War phase, mainly in the years between 1956 and 1974. Then there was a lull until the late 1980s, when, with the end of the Cold War, there was a sudden revival of demand and very rapid growth.

A. U.N. PEACEKEEPING OPERATIONS
DURING THE COLD WAR

During the Cold War phase, peacekeeping was fairly homogeneous. It had become a fairly well-defined activity, though never formally defined in a resolution of the Security Council, let alone in the Charter. There were certain essential characteristics recognized and accepted by everybody.

First of all, these were operations by the United Nations. They were under the command and control of the Secretary-General, who was responsible to the Security Council. They were financed collectively by the Member-States as activities of the organization.

Secondly, peacekeeping operations were only set up with the consent of the parties to the conflict in question.

Thirdly, peacekeepers had to be impartial between the two sides. They were not there to promote the interests of one side against those of the other.

Fourthly, the troops involved were provided voluntarily by Member-States to the Secretary-General at his request.

Fifthly, those peacekeeping operations which were armed (only a minority were armed) were authorized to use force only in self-defense. But—and this is a very important "but"—from the early 1970s, self-defense had been deemed to include situations in which armed persons were trying, by force, to prevent the peacekeepers from carrying out their orders. There is a great deal of misunderstanding around the world today about the rules of engagement of peacekeeping. It is often said that the peacekeepers have their hands tied behind their backs by UN rules, UN procedures. That is not the case. What ties the peacekeepers' hands behind their backs, what causes them to hesitate to use force, are the decisions of their commanders on the spot—the knowledge of the commanders that, in a situation where you are supposed to be impartial, if you start using force, you are going to lose the cooperation of one of the parties, on whose cooperation your operation depends. This reluctance to use force also reflects the fact that the troops are deployed with armament and in numbers based on the assumption that the parties are going to cooperate with them. So if you are thinking about the forceful application of the will of the Security Council, you've got to deploy a quite different force—different in armament, different in command structures—from the force which you deploy for peacekeeping purposes.

Finally, these Cold War peacekeeping operations were, in almost all cases, interim arrangements—almost entirely military in composition and in mandate—intended to control or prevent a resumption of fighting to allow space and time for the diplomats, the negotiators, the peacemakers, to work out a peaceful, agreed settlement of the dispute.

B. VARIED TYPES OF POST-COLD WAR OPERATIONS

Since 1988, peacekeeping has evolved very rapidly in the post-Cold War situation. Whereas before it was, as I said, a fairly homogeneous activity, one can now identify six or seven different types of operations. They vary considerably, in ways which have important consequences for the way they should be commanded, the way they should be manned, the way they should be armed.

1. Preventive Deployment (Macedonia)

The first type is what we call preventive deployment, an idea which came originally from Mikhail Gorbachev and was developed in the Secretary-General's report called *An Agenda for Peace*. The idea is that, in a potentially threatening situation, the United Nations, at the request of one of the parties to the potential conflict, would deploy troops, as a confidence-building measure and also as a measure which would raise the political price if the potential aggressor were to attack the other party. We have only one example, Macedonia. There is no conflict going on in Macedonia at present, but there is a great deal of concern that there might be a conflict there, and we have deployed a battalion of troops and some military observers and some civilian policemen as a preventive deployment.

2. Traditional Peacekeeping (Near East, Kashmir, Cyprus, Iraq-Kuwait, Croatia)

The second type of peacekeeping operation is traditional peacekeeping, what I have described as Cold War peacekeeping—the largely military operation, deployed as an interim arrangement to control fighting while peacemaking negotiation takes place. There are three sub-types.

One is the unarmed military observer group. The first peacekeeping operation ever, in the Near East in 1948, was (and still is) an unarmed military observer group.

Second are armed infantry-based forces, used when one needs to control territory—a buffer zone or a demilitarized zone from which the forces of the two sides have agreed to withdraw. You need an armed force, both symbolically and to control small incidents. We have those in Cyprus, in Syria, in southern Lebanon, in Croatia. Sometimes people complain that the armed force which is successfully controlling a buffer zone is becoming part of the problem. It's an argument you often hear in the case of Cyprus. The UN force has been there for 29 years. People say, "Take it away and maybe the two sides will come to their senses—maybe they can be persuaded to negotiate a settlement." I personally think that's a very bad argument. First of all, if you took the force away it would almost certainly re-ignite fighting in Cyprus. Secondly, it's contrary to the whole philosophy of the United Nations, which is to settle disputes peacefully, not by the use (or the threat of the use) of force.

The third sub-type is an operation set up as a consequence of peace-enforcement. The only example at present is the observer mission we have on the border between Iraq and Kuwait. Iraq was, in effect, obliged at the end of Desert Storm to accept that deployment, but it has nevertheless been operated in accordance with the standard principles of peacekeeping.

3. Helping Implement Negotiated Agreements (Namibia, Cambodia, Angola, Mozambique, El Salvador)

Type three (of which there was one example in the Cold War period, a small and forgotten operation in West Irian) are operations which are set up, for a specified period of time, to help previously hostile parties implement an agreement which has been negotiated between them. This is a new type of peacekeeping operation. To a considerable extent, the new demand for peacekeeping resulted from the success which we had in this kind of operation in Namibia, where, after a decade of negotiation, agreement was reached. The United Nations put in a large force. In less than a year it helped the two sides, South Africa and SWAPO (the Namibian national liberation movement), to implement their agreement. It was a great success, and it still is a great success. We have had less success in Angola, where the operation has gone badly wrong. We are carrying out this sort of operation in El Salvador, in Cambodia, and are just starting in Mozambique.

4. Protecting Delivery of Humanitarian Supplies (Bosnia-Herzegovina, Somalia)

Type four, again a new type, is the deployment of UN troops to protect the delivery of humanitarian supplies, in civil war or inter-state war situations. It was a possibility that had been very much discussed in academic circles, and it became real last year in Somalia and in Bosnia and Herzegovina. It has turned out to be an extremely difficult operation because you are trying to combine two things: You are trying to combine the famous impartiality of peacekeeping with the promotion of activities which may be against the war objectives of one (or perhaps both) of the warring parties. The efforts of the United Nations, in peacekeeping mode, to deliver humanitarian supplies to Muslim populations in Bosnia-Herzegovina are against the war objectives of the Bosnian Serbs—and are therefore constantly blocked by the Bosnian Serbs.

In Somalia it was a different situation. It was a situation of total lawlessness, where it became quite quickly clear that peacekeeping was not going to work. It was therefore necessary to move from peacekeeping (something done with the consent of the parties) to peace enforcement, initially via a force put together by the United States—now the United Nations is taking over that function.

Already here in type four we are moving out of peacekeeping into something which is close to peace enforcement—may indeed be peace enforcement. This blurring of the line, this creation of a gray area between peacekeeping and peace enforcement, is potentially a very hazardous thing. In Somalia, and to some extent in Bosnia-Herzegovina, we have deployed troops armed and commanded in a way in which peacekeeping troops are armed and commanded; and it has turned out that that is not sufficient for the humanitarian supplies to get through. Equally, for the military mind, fighting the humanitarian supplies through is a rather daunting concept, especially in a country where the terrain and the climate are as difficult as in the former Yugoslavia.

5. "Painting a Country Blue" (Somalia)

Type five is what Douglas Hurd recently called "painting a country blue." The United Nations moves into a country which is in a state of total disorder, where the institutions of government have collapsed, where nothing is working, where there is no political authority with which one can successfully negotiate. The United Nations did it once during the Cold War period—in the Congo in the early 1960s. Whatever we may think of President Mobutu now, it was a successful operation during four years—though at considerable cost, including the life of the then Secretary-General. The United Nations did succeed in putting the Congo together again as an effective, working state.

That is what we are going to do now in Somalia. The task in Somalia is not just the delivery of humanitarian supplies; it is—to some extent—taking charge of Somalia during a period in which we will be promoting a process of national reconciliation between the many different factions. Meanwhile, we are finding that we have to provide all sorts of governmental services—like a police force for instance, which is not normally something which United Nations peacekeepers have to do.

It may be that the same kind of task will fall to us in Bosnia, if the Vance-Owen plan is accepted by all the parties and the United Nations goes in with a very large presence to help implement that plan.

6. Cease-Fire Enforcement

The sixth type is something which the Secretary-General, in *An Agenda for Peace*, called "peace enforcement," though "cease-fire enforcement" is perhaps a more accurate way of describing it. We have not done this yet. We may do it in Bosnia. You have a cease-fire (signed by the two sides in a war) but then one side or the other (or both) fails to respect the cease-fire. The United Nations troops would go in with a mandate to use force against anyone who breaks the cease-fire. If there is a cease-fire in Sarajevo and the Serb artillery continues to shell the city, then United Nations troops would silence that Serb artillery. They would be impartial, unlike, say, in Desert Storm or Korea. They would not be fighting for one side against the other. They would be impartial between the two sides, but they would use force against anybody who violated the cease-fire. It is a very demanding concept militarily. It's not peacekeeping at all really—if you compare it with the characteristics of Cold War peacekeeping that I described, this is something very different. But it's the way in which the activity may develop.

7. Peace Enforcement (Kuwait)

I suppose, for completeness' sake, I should mention a type seven. This is peace enforcement—the use of international forces in a war to support the good guy and stop the bad guy's aggression, as in Korea and Kuwait. In both those cases, the troops were not under the command of the Secretary-General; they were under the command of national authorities who had been authorized by the Security Council to use force for a specific purpose.

C. STEPS NEEDED FOR RAPID EXPANSION NOT TO UNDERMINE WHOLE ACTIVITY

After that attempt to describe the complexity and varied nature of "peacekeeping" at present, I would now like to address three problems which arise from this rapid expansion: finance, management, and priorities.

1. Adequate Finance

As far as finance is concerned, the answers are set out very clearly in Enid Schoettle's excellent chapter in the draft report (and in the report of the Independent Advisory Group on U.N. Financing chaired by Paul Volcker and Shijuro Ogata). It's not a particularly difficult problem to provide the necessary finance for peacekeeping. The sums involved—though they seem frightening by comparison with foreign ministry budgets or the regular budget of the United Nations Secretariat—are not enormous sums when compared with what nations spend on defense. It's a matter of political decision. It's a matter of governments matching their readiness to set up new peacekeeping operations with a readiness to provide the necessary finance.

There is a certain amount which the Secretariat needs to do. In some of these things we need the cooperation of the Member-States also—for instance, modernizing our very antiquated and sclerotic financial procedures. We need to clean up our own house and make sure that Member-States who contribute money for peacekeeping can be confident that their money will be used effectively and honestly.

2. Radically Strengthened Management Capability

Management is a bigger problem. Everyone now agrees that the United Nations Secretariat's structures for commanding, controlling, and managing peacekeeping operations are lamentably inadequate. Although everybody recognizes that, governments have not so far been ready to provide the Secretary-General with the additional resources that he needs. The watchword amongst the Member-States is "re-deployment." If more staff are needed to support peacekeeping, then they must be found from within the existing staff, from lower-priority activities of the United Nations. I had a painful afternoon a few weeks ago when I asked for eight additional military staff in my old department. After an afternoon of being cross-questioned by the representatives of some very senior members of the Security Council about why this was really necessary, I was told, well, I could have two extra officers but only for six months. So, there is a "disconnect" between the readiness of Member-States to set up peacekeeping operations, the recognition of Member-States that we haven't got the structures to do it right at present, and their reluctance—or the reluctance of their staff who work on financial questions—to make the additional resources available. As a result, we have been forced into some makeshift arrangements which have not been entirely satisfactory. We have perforce had to accept offers of staff by Member-States. The same Member-States who may be difficult about increasing our own resources offer us officers and civilian officials free of charge (the individual Member-State will pay). That is a bad arrangement because those officers and those civil servants tend to report back to their own governments before we are ready to share information with them.

In the field, when it was decided that we needed to expand substantially the operation in Bosnia-Herzegovina for the protection of humanitarian supplies, given the urgency and given the inadequacy of our own planning staffs and so on, it was decided to sub-contract both the planning for that operation and the provision of the headquarters in the field to NATO. Elements of a NATO headquarters, from the Northern Army Group, were taken off the shelf and deployed to Bosnia-Herzegovina. One's disquiet about this is not just a matter of UN *amour-propre*. The real problem with that kind of solution is that the Secretary-General loses control of the operation. The activities of the command in Bosnia-Herzegovina at present are not in any real sense under the control of the Secretary-General, or even under the control of the overall commander of the

UN forces in the former Yugoslavia. This has quite severe consequences because it undermines the credibility of this operation as a truly multinational operation, as an expression of the will of the international community.

Olara Otunnu, in his chapter, writes wisely about the necessity for UN peacekeeping operations to be perceived as legitimate by the Member-States as a whole, by the international community as a whole. If they come to be seen as something which is done, in effect, by a Western military alliance, they will lose that legitimacy. That may sound surprising in a Trilateral context. But if you are sitting in New York with 180 delegations, it is a striking phenomenon which policymakers need to take into account.

The solution which I personally advocate—like all this speech, this is a personal view—is that we radically revise the concept for the planning and the command and control of UN peacekeeping operations at United Nations headquarters in New York. We should establish a general staff, mainly military but including civilian officials as well, which will do two things: It will do the planning for new operations, and it will provide the core elements for the headquarters in the field. This would have the advantage of strengthening our planning capability, and also ensure that, when we send a new force out, those who plan it will go out to set up the headquarters and provide the core elements in the headquarters. That gives us better command and control, and it means also that the established principles and procedures and practices of peacekeeping would be applied uniformly in all the different operations. Establishing such a general staff is a very difficult thing to achieve, because you are talking about recruiting, I would think, several hundred—maybe as many as five hundred—additional staff to work in New York on this activity. A lot of them we would have to recruit as military officers, in mid-career: Staff-trained officers of proven ability with some previous experience in UN peacekeeping service would be invited, in their late 30s or early 40s, to sign on to work with the United Nations as soldiers. In the Cold War that would have been a totally unacceptable concept, because the Russians would never agree to the Secretary-General having any kind of military capability, not even a military staff. I think now it may be possible. We would have to do all sorts of things to our staff rules and our contract system and so on, but I believe that is the way forward.

3. Security Council Priorities

Finally, on priorities, all of us in the Secretariat feel that the Security Council needs to be a little more careful, a little more reflective, before it decides where to deploy peacekeeping operations. This is for three reasons.

First is the financial reason. There are not unlimited resources available for peacekeeping.

Second is credibility. The current credibility of United Nations peacekeeping is based on some successes, especially the success in Namibia. That credibility will be very rapidly undermined if we have some conspicuous failures. We have had one in Angola already. We may be going to have one in Cambodia (though personally I am fairly optimistic about Cambodia). Another Angola or two would very seriously undermine credibility. It therefore behooves the Security Council to take care to put peacekeeping operations only into situations where there is a reasonable prospect that peacekeeping is going to work.

Third is the question of management capability—what I was talking about a moment ago. It is going to take us time to get our own house in order and establish the capacity to plan and to command and control peacekeeping operations on the scale at present deployed and envisaged.

This places a great burden of responsibility on the Secretary-General. He is the guardian or the trustee of a resource—peacekeeping—which has been very carefully nurtured over the years, and whose credibility depends on it being seen to be successful.

Preserving that credibility is no easy task. It's very difficult for the Secretary-General. On the one hand, he has to try to ensure that peacekeepers are not deployed in conditions where failure is likely. On the other hand, he has to avoid appearing so cautious as to create doubts about the real usefulness of the United Nations or to provide a pretext for Member-States to go back to their wicked old unilateral ways.

This is not a responsibility which the Secretary-General should be asked to share alone. The power of decision rests with the Security Council; and it's important that the members of the Council if necessary, stand up to the clamor from their electorates—stand up to the regional clamor—and take care to satisfy themselves, in advance, that conditions really exist for a proposed peacekeeping operation to succeed.

Those conditions are well-known, but I would like, in conclusion, to repeat them: (1) the mandate or task of the peacekeeping operation must be clear, practicable and accepted by the parties; (2) the parties must pledge themselves to cooperate with the peacekeepers and those pledges must be credible; (3) the Member-States of the United Nations must be ready to provide the human and material resources needed to do the job. Unfortunately, on any particular day only a minority of the actual or potential conflicts in the world fulfill those conditions. It's often very frustrating to have to wait until a conflict is ripe for the UN peacekeeping treatment before deploying the peacekeepers. But if the conditions are fulfilled, if the conditions are right, then there is almost no limit to what the peacekeepers can achieve.